PROTESTANT PANORAMA

The Cathedral of Democracy. Christ Church, in Philadelphia, founded on November 15, 1695, was for years the church home of many of America's Founding Fathers. Today a popular shrine of historical mementos, Christ Church was planned by the same architects who were associated with the building of Independence Hall. From its pulpit in Colonial days came summonses to freedom and independence that powerfully affected the thinking and action of the patriots. The above color-photo, made especially for **PROTESTANT PANORAMA** by Arthur H. d'Arazien, shows a congregation at worship.

PROTESTANT PANORAMA

A STORY OF THE FAITH THAT MADE AMERICA FREE

by Clarence W. Hall and Desider Holisher

WITH AN INTRODUCTION BY CHARLES P. TAFT

FARRAR, STRAUS AND YOUNG · NEW YORK

CONTENTS

Introduction: Charles P. Taft vii

Prelude: Origin of the "Big Idea" 3

I Our American Heritage 9

II The Protestant at Worship 23

III The Protestant Layman 49

IV Ten Million Church Women 63

V "Young America" at Its Best 75

VI Unity within Diversity 91

VII Protestant Design and Social Disorder 109

VIII "With All Thy Mind" 127

IX Propagators of the Word 147

X World Outreach 161

Postlude: "An Idea Whose Time Has Come" 174

Acknowledgments 177

Bibliography 179

INTRODUCTION

BY CHARLES P. TAFT

The idea that every person is a child of God entitled to exercise free choices for life and action, limited only by community pressure against crime and by voluntary consideration for your neighbor, has been a revolutionary and explosive concept. It drove our ancestors to these shores and spread them from ocean to ocean, while leaving the seeds of peaceful change behind in the old countries.

It is human, I suppose, to become defensive about the success achieved under that driving force, but it is both wrong and bad strategy. We need to search our national past and our individual experience for the dynamic that brought us Americans to this point, and we need to renew its beneficial and explosive force for further advance, even though it means change that upsets our comfort and our complacency.

The core and origin of the free choices by which we live is religious liberty. The urge of the underdog to rise, when unleavened by our Jewish-Christian tradition, becomes the hate and envy of the Marxist, and reaches its inevitable climax in the cruel fanaticism of the Kremlin.

Religious liberty and the dramatic participation of our American freedom finds its modern origin in turn in the vigorous religious thinking that boiled up in England from the Reformation through the seventeenth century. We need a much more intelligent understanding of these foundations and the growth from them. That must come from a fresh study of the basic elements of the Reformation.

The beginning point is the Scriptures which contain everything necessary for salvation, as the Anglican Articles put it. It is extraordinary that a library like the Bible, put together during five centuries just before and after Christ, should meet the varying needs of so many generations living in so many centuries. The scholars of the great Protestant and Orthodox communions, working today under the World Council of Churches, are finding new meanings in the old Book for our urban industrial civilization.

The Reformers renewed the conviction that God is waiting for man's approach to him in faith, and proclaimed that every person who sought, could reach Him without intervention of priest, or saint, or church, or any but Christ himself. This conviction brought two results, one that when God spoke in one's heart and conscience, one must speak and do His will; and a humility, too, in the end, for God *might* be speaking through some other sincere Christian who had sought him also.

This freedom to judge in one's conscience and obligation to speak and do God's will, based on that judgment, is the heart and the dynamic of our culture of free choices and democratic participation. Since its modern form grew out of the Reformation and Protestantism, Protestants must understand it better and proclaim it. They had better be less defensive and fearful, and garner more of the affirmative enthusiasm of this book.

For instance, they need not be so disturbed about our diversities and differences of opinion, so long as they are displayed in Christian love and forbearance.

Protestants need to be much more interested in how to apply Christian principles in daily life and less worried about even "pink fringes" in the church. The Christian religion is a religion of perfection which must subject every act and condition to moral scrutiny, and measure it against Christ's standard to produce a divine discontent and a determination to improve.

At the same time all of us have to struggle in a world of evil and death, and the tough fibre of Protestantism must be recovered from much of the soft sentimentality that has sometimes engulfed us. The fight for freedom against the absolutism of earlier centuries needs all the iron of the backbone that we inherit from the great Reformers. We thought we had won that fight but we find it renewed in unprecedented fanaticism.

Yet in the fire of the new struggles we shall, if we cling to our religious traditions, emerge cleansed of the dross we have accumulated, and with a fresh power to promote the freedom we cherish.

PROTESTANT PANORAMA

1

ORIGIN OF THE "BIG IDEA"

This is the story of Protestantism in the United States. Not a definitive study, it is rather a panoramic view, a sweeping look at Protestantism as it is today. It is also a reminder to Protestants of the heritage that is theirs, of the part—the tremendous part—their faith has played and is playing in the life of our country, its development and culture.

If, as John C. Miller asserts in his *Origins of the American Revolution,* it is true that "the chief source of spiritual nourishment for any nation must be its own past, perpetually rediscovered and renewed," then American Protestants need to know about their faith, its scope and its origin. They need to see not only its present fruits but its early roots. The prime thing all Americans, of whatever faith, need to know is just this: *The American heritage is the Protestant heritage!* For, more than anything else, it was Protestantism's religious and social ideals that founded and have preserved the democratic way of life as we know it and as we practice it.

What, precisely, is Protestantism, and where did it come from? What is its peculiar genius, and whence its particular genesis?

First, let us be clear as to what it is *not.* Protestantism is not a church. There is but one Christian Church, and all denominations or sects are but branches. Essentially, Protestantism is an idea, a spirit. It is a way of thinking God's thoughts after Him. It is a way of thinking about man, his dignity and rights as an individual, his potentialities and his powers.

Protestantism is not, fundamentally, a "protest" against anything. Its accent has ever been on the positive, the affirmative. "Protestant" comes from the Latin roots *pro* (meaning "for") and *testari* ("to be a witness"). It signifies those who testify *for* something; it stands for those who have made an avowal about something important. That something is an idea—capitalize it, a Big Idea—which God has for ages been trying to plant in the mind and heart of man.

Reach for a one-word description of this Big Idea that is Protestantism's prime genius, and what do you come up with? To save your soul, you cannot avoid one word: *freedom.* Thus . . .

(1) Protestantism is *Freedom of Conscience:* the right and responsibility of every man, in his stature and dignity as an individual created in the image of God, to worship as his conscience dictates, to make his own judgments and not be coerced into them, and to be responsible for those judgments.

(2) Protestantism is *Freedom of Grace:* with salvation the free gift of God, not to be earned by good deeds, not to be purchased with the coin of any realm.

(3) Protestantism is *Freedom of Access to God:* requiring no mediator save Christ, estab-

lishing irretrievably the priesthood of every believer.

(4) Protestantism is *Freedom of Religion from Authoritarian Control:* the vigorous denial to any government, whether political or ecclesiastical or both, of the right to dictate, underwrite or establish a "state faith" to which all must adhere.

Protestantism, pure and undefiled, is the most democratic thing on earth today. Define it as you will, you cannot separate it from the Big Idea of Liberty. Wherever it goes, it breaks men's chains, imparts freedom of soul and mind and body, lifts men in all their God-given rights as sons of God to new and ever more creative patterns of social and spiritual responsibility.

A faith, any faith, is known by the company it keeps. Protestantism has always been associated with free men, free societies. When there was no freedom, it made men free; in the midst of slave states, it has nurtured the growth of the free society.

It is this Big Idea of freedom that Protestantism stands for. Basically religious, it glimmers to some extent in most creeds. But Protestantism has made it basic, setting it at the foundation, building upon it as the cornerstone. It is not surprising, therefore, that Protestants came to America, settled America, made America after the likeness of their own ideal. Freedom, given half a chance, will reproduce itself. That is why, sparked by Protestant America, freedom is the ideal inflaming the world today, setting afire the minds of little people everywhere, starting them on the march to self-realization, God-realization.

But where, precisely, did Protestantism begin? Some would have you think it began with John the Baptist heralding the coming of the Redeemer on the banks of the Jordan. Or with angry Martin Luther hammering his theses onto the Wittenberg door. Or with the lusty and loutish Henry VIII wanting to rid himself of one queen to take another. Churches, as branches of Christendom, may or may not have had such origins. But not Protestantism.

Protestantism began with the Big Idea itself. And that takes you back to "Our fathers' God . . . Author of Liberty." It takes you back, clear back, to the creation of man, whom God made in His own likeness, made free to roam and replenish the earth, made free to decide how or even whether he would serve his Creator. It takes you back to Moses, shaking his fist in Pharaoh's face and crying: "Let my people go!" and forthwith leading a great army of the enslaved into a new and free country where he would "proclaim liberty throughout the land and to all the inhabitants thereof."*

It takes you back to the Old Testament prophets, proclaiming in the face of wrathful kings and shouting from dungeons and prisons man's inalienable right to liberty. Look at the Jew. To tyrants of all ages, he has always been a puzzle and a snare. God had put something in him that made him unsalable on any auction block. Even the Romans, adept at the slavery business, had to give up; they said: "There's something in his fanatical religion that makes him useless as a slave."

It takes you back to the Son of God who, standing in the Nazareth synagogue, cast into the scheming faces of religious bigots and Roman tyrants the bold declaration of His destiny: "The Lord hath anointed Me to preach deliverance to the captives, to set at liberty them that are bruised!"

It takes you back to Paul, who lighted his torch from a converting flame on the Damascus Road and flung that torch across the world. Paul it was, Jew and Roman citizen, who

---

* Spoken by Jehovah to Moses on Mt. Sinai, these words are found in Leviticus 25:10—and, with powerful pertinence, on America's Liberty Bell.

organized and universalized the Christian Church. In a day when slavery and subjection were the rule, Paul spoke of the "glorious liberty of the children of God." To slaves and masters alike, he dared to declare: "Where the spirit of the Lord is, there is liberty." To jailed and jailers alike, he boasted of "the liberty wherewith Christ hath made us free." And to one and all, he cried: "Brethren, ye have been called unto liberty!"

Liberty, freedom . . . freedom, liberty! These were the challenging, inflaming, revolutionary words these forerunners of American·Protestantism cast again and again into the tinderbox that was mankind's heart and imagination. The Early Church held these words to their hearts, preached them fearlessly and died in the preaching, wrought them into their early literature and preserved them in the souls of generation after generation. They had a firm hold on the Big Idea, these saints and martyrs, and they would not let it go. The teeth of lions could not tear it from them, torture racks could not wrench it from their hearts, martyr fires could not burn it away. "We must obey God rather than man!" they cried—and died. But the cry itself soared out and away to hover like a banner over those who arose to take their place.

It was not the Christians' *piety* that the earth's tyrants feared. It was this ideal of the Free Man in God. That ideal is always terrifying to tyrants, of whatever era or complexion or denomination.

Augustus, the first Roman Emperor, sagacious pagan, tried to combat it by substitution. Men must worship? Then let them worship Caesar! Thus was adopted the age-old "divine right of kings," a notion that was to plague Christians for generations. Constantine, at the beginning of the Fourth Century, tried to contain the Big Idea by amalgamation: he made Christianity "official," thus creating the first alliance of Church and State and injecting into the Church's bloodstream a poison that was to infect it for sixteen hundred years.

Then came the real Dark Ages of the Big Idea—the centuries when self-appointed leaders of the Church, softly wrapped in the smothering folds of the purple, sold its liberty and freedom for the pottage of state support. Intolerance set in and solidified, and men were told: "Worship this way or be damned!" Corruption spread, and there arose a long and disgraceful line of religious despots who cared more for their own license than the people's liberty, more for their shekels than the people's shackles. For those who tried to throw off their chains, there was the butchery of the Inquisition.

It was a bleak time for the Big Idea. Nevertheless, the Idea had its champions—even then, even there. There was Thomas Aquinas who preached the supremacy of conscience. There was John Wyclif, "morning star of the Reformation," who led a people's revolt against papal aggressions in England, and who put into the hands of his countrymen the first New Testament written in English. There was John Huss of Bohemia, who led an uprising against clerical landlords who owned one-third of the land, and who was burned at the stake by them. There was Erasmus the Hollander, who cried for a new day when every man would be his own priest, carrying his own altar in his own heart. These were no riffraff, no "come-outers" at heart. They were scholars and gentlemen of the first rank. These and other stalwarts were staging what Lord Morley has described as "an insurrection against the base and demoralizing surrender of the individual: the surrender of his understanding to the church, of his conscience to the priest, of his will to the prince."

The Bible, by hook or by crook, was getting

around, despite all efforts to keep its revolutionary ideas chained. And gradually, as they read, the common people discovered that the Bible's truths were not at all beyond their comprehension, as they had been told. Waldensians in Italy and France, Lollards in England, Hussites in Bohemia read for themselves and marveled at what they read. They began to see such words as "liberty" and "free grace," and they began to catch the tremendous implications behind those words.

Everywhere, in obscure little places and right amid the carnal center of an ecclesiastical system gone wrong, the Big Idea was at work, putting banners in men's hands, tuning the trumpets of freedom for a major advance.

And then came Martin Luther, loudest trumpeter of them all. An Augustinian monk, angry to the core at clerical oppression and lust for power and gold, he took one long look at the high-pressure "indulgences" salesmen sent into his parish by Pope Leo X, the Medici banker, and seized his trumpet. Accompaniment for the blast he sounded was the thud of his nails through the theses on the Wittenberg door. And when he rode to Worms to face the Diet called to make him recant, in that cart, on that most electric day in Reformation history, rode Liberty coming into her own.

We would not claim too much for Luther. Reform was on the rise in many places before he came on the scene and after he left it. Yet it was his mighty trumpet that set the pitch for the fuller orchestration being sounded everywhere.

A fiery young priest named Huldreich Zwingli blew a blast in Switzerland, and died on a battlefield red with the blood of warring Catholics and Protestants. John Calvin succeeded him in Geneva, and became the creator of the nonconformist conscience and the founder of the Puritan strain. Lean and hard and uncompromising, Calvin trumpeted the "Sovereignty of God" theme that set to marching an army of freedom's iron men. Calvin's disciples scattered all over Europe. And wherever they went, they started men's hearts beating high with liberty's hopes. They supplied the backbone of the Dutch revolt against Spanish and Catholic domination; they spilled into France and became part of the Huguenots and their gallant fight; they flowed into Scotland and rallied behind John Knox in his defiance of the Catholic Queen of Scots. We owe a lot to the Calvinists!

In England, long before Henry VIII made his switch in wives and faith, the Big Idea was being spread by the "Oxford Reformers." Puritanism there too became a movement constantly mounting through the generations. And despite the bloody opposition of Catholic Mary and the later and more refined threats of Anglican Elizabeth, there began to appear, outside the Established Church and in protest over its dodo-deadness, such strange new names as "Congregationalist," "Presbyterian," "Quaker," "Baptist." Many others with freedom and reform singing in their souls remained Anglicans, and gave themselves to purifying the Church from within. Badgered, repressed, sneered at, they were driven from pillar to post. Some went to Holland; some to other parts of the Continent, where they joined with others in the brotherhood of those on the hunt for religious liberty.

And some, seeing in prophetic vision a new "nation under God" that could be "conceived in liberty and dedicated to the proposition that all men are created equal," clambered aboard a tiny vessel one chill day in 1620 and, with prayers on their lips, set sail for a far, strange land. The name carved on the prow of their little ship was *The Mayflower*.

The Big Idea was on its way to the New World . . .

One of the noblest ventures for religious faith and for civil liberty was demonstrated by the little band of the Pilgrims, whose heroic enterprise is immortalized in numerous artistic creations. The huge painting by Robert W. Weir, "Embarkation of the Pilgrims," seen in the rotunda of the Capitol in Washington, D.C., and a duplicate of it in Pilgrim Hall, Plymouth, Mass., depicts dramatically their first prayer on the deck of their ship.

The National Monument to the Forefathers, towering high above the Plymouth (Mass.) harbor, symbolizes the lofty ideals the Pilgrim left to posterity. In the above the mighty figure of Faith, with the Bible in her hand, raises her right arm to point to heaven. Smaller figures at the base signify the principles for which the Pilgrims stood and on which America was established: Liberty, Morality, Law and Education. At the base are marble groups depicting episodes in the Pilgrim undertaking, most significant of which was the signing of the Compact aboard the "Mayflower," a momentous document of American history.

I

OUR AMERICAN HERITAGE

It mattered little, in those days of our country's beginnings, *how* you came or when. It mattered greatly *why* you came and what you brought with you.

Christopher Columbus set sail for the New World a century and a quarter ahead of the Pilgrims. In the hearts of those aboard his tiny flotilla burned the lust for gold and high adventure. The winds in the sails of the *Santa Maria* whispered of fabulous wealth and a new empire for their Roman Catholic Majesties, Ferdinand and Isabella. Columbus failed; he never set foot on the mainland, and when he died in Spain, he was a discredited and disillusioned man.

Magellan and Balboa and Cortez, Ponce de Leon and de Soto and Coronado also came. They waded ashore with sword in hand, missionary priests trailing behind. The priests were good men and heroic. But both they and the conquerors they accompanied failed. New Spain perished quickly, and virtually the only monuments left by the priests are a few ancient mission bells tolling the requiem of their venture.

Roman Catholic France also had a try at it. Along with her gay voyageurs came the Jesuits, who swarmed in to capture the New World for the Roman Church while the explorers were capturing vast areas for France. The missionary zeal of the Jesuits was noteworthy. But

they failed, so far as that part of the New World now comprising the United States was concerned, and they disappeared.

Why? Why did all these brave and ambitious forerunners of the Pilgrims fail? Was it not because they were tied to systems, governmental and ecclesiastic, which were forever alien to this new land? It was as though Almighty God had scrolled across these free skies: "Abandon hope all ye who enter here, save as ye enter to establish that liberty wherewith Christ hath set men free!"

Even the Cavaliers and Royalists from England, setting up their colony in Jamestown, found the going tough and would have perished had it not been for the coming of their countrymen with higher goals than the acquisition of far-flung plantations and aristocratic ease. The Jamestowners had no specially flaming notions about religious liberty—except for liberty to transplant the Church of England and force every colonist into its groove.

Then, long decades in the wake of the *Santa Maria,* came the gallant little *Mayflower.* Her sails were bellied out with the winds of freedom, and she was loaded to the gunwales with a different kind of explorer. They were explorers of the spirit, those 102 Calvinists, Separatists, Dissenters. In their bones burned a thirst for freedom, in their hearts a faith that was more adventure than creed. In their hands

Roger Williams, fiery young Baptist refugee, brought to the colonies a demand that liberty, religious and civil, must be for red man and white, believer and unbeliever, dissenter and sectarian.

was the Bible, the Textbook of Freedom, containing the chart and compass of their dream. Hymn writer Leonard Bacon inventoried their luggage: "Laws, freedom, truth and faith in God came with those exiles o'er the waves!"

The night before that historic dawn when they rushed to the *Mayflower's* rails to get their first sight of the New World, they had crowded into her tiny hold to write their "Mayflower Compact," later to be called "the birth certificate of American democracy." That compact, sweated out in prayer, read: "In the name of God, Amen; We, whose names are underwritten, for the glory of God and advancement of the Christian faith . . . do, in the presence of God and one another, covenant and combine ourselves into a Civil Body Politic, for

our better ordering and preservation, and furtherance of the ends aforesaid."

And the Puritans who followed during the great immigration of 1630-40 likewise laid on the line their reasons for coming to Massachusetts Bay. The opening sentence of their "New England Confederation" says: "We all came into these parts of America with one and the same end, namely, to advance the Kingdom of the Lord Jesus Christ."

Not all, of course, were pious. There crowded in with the Puritans a host of adventurers, ex-prisoners, unbelievers. But it is a mark of the Puritans' and the Pilgrims' vitality that their ideas and ideals prevailed over those who came for reasons other than conscience.

The Pilgrims and the Puritans stayed! The

William Penn followed his Quaker's "inner light" to found in Pennsylvania and New Jersey colonies that are among America's noblest memorials to the proper relation between religion and statecraft.

American Dream, highest political fulfilment to date of the Big Idea, was firmly planted. Down, deep down, went the roots, and nothing has been able to tear them out. Moderns may scoff at the Puritan's straitlacedness, carp at his early intolerance. But they should never forget that the Puritan's religion, his concept of equality and passion for self-rule, gave us our system of political and social democracy.

True enough, the Puritan did not spring overnight into his full stature as a religious freeman. He had come to America for freedom of conscience—his *own* freedom for his *own* conscience. Concerning other men's consciences, he was stern and bigoted for a time. It is the history of the hunted and the persecuted that, upon suddenly gaining freedom, they tend to

think only of their own freedom. But, mark this, a man cannot embrace this liberty without, in time, embracing all others; he cannot deny it without, in time, denying all other freedoms. Once the Puritan had sunk his roots in the principle, the full plant and flower was inevitable.

From the Puritan, main stalk of American democracy, new shoots began to appear, new plants to arise. Most important of all was Roger Williams. A gallant rebel on the run from King James's wrath, this fiery young Baptist hit the Massachusetts Bay Colony in 1631 like a thrashing tornado. They called him "passionate, precipitate and divinely mad." Cotton Mather sized him up as a man "with a windmill in his mind." But mostly in Williams' mind were the

First act of the colonists upon arriving in the New World was the erection of a meeting-house, reli- **gious and social center of the colony, bastion of both their spiritual and civil liberties.**

vaulting ideas on religious liberty later given voice in England by Puritan John Locke.

Roger Williams saw the Bay Colony as a theocracy, with a state religion quite as intolerant as that from which he had fled. He wanted no part of a religion officially appointed, officially supported. He became the first champion of "separation of Church and State." When the theocrats sought to expel him, he fled to found Providence, R. I., a city for dissenters, a

city set high on a hill with every street open to the breezes of religious freedom, no matter from what quarter they blew. Not alone to Christians, but to Jews also, he offered freedom of faith. To make it stick he put down on paper and implemented in his colony specific guarantees of civil and religious freedom— many of them embodied a hundred years later in our national Bill of Rights.

We owe a lot to this man with a windmill

Old Ship Church, at Hingham, Mass., was established in 1630. Its present building, erected in 1681, is the oldest church structure in the United States to have been used continuously for worship.

in his mind. As Frank S. Mead has said: "Martin Luther gave us the right to be *Protestant;* Roger Williams gave us the right to be *any kind of Protestant."*

No offshoot of Puritanism was William Penn. He was a sturdy stalk of his own growing—and God's. Son of a fighting British admiral, Penn was the spiritual son of George Fox, fighting Quaker. For his faith Penn had borne blows and prison bars. Soft-spoken and a lover of peace, he nevertheless was an aggressive believer in free religion. Shaking the dust of England from his brogans and following his Inner Light, Penn led his Friends into what is now Pennsylvania and New Jersey. And the colonies he founded are among America's noblest memorials to the proper relation between religion and statecraft. You can see the hand of Penn in the Great Law of Pennsylvania, which, passed in December, 1682, declared: "The glory of

Almighty God, and the good of mankind, is the reason and end of government, and, therefore, government in itself is a venerable ordinance of God."

The Dutch purchased Manhattan Island for twenty-four dollars and there planted their Reformed Church. Swedes and Germans brought a string of Lutheran churches to the banks of the Delaware. Oglethorpe helped the Moravians to settle in Georgia, then went back to London to walk the streets with a half-dozen Indians he had brought along; interested John and Charles Wesley, and took them back with him. Some Huguenots, scattered over other parts of the South, and Scots brought their staunch Presbyterianism into the middle colonies. America soon was the land of the religiously free, home of the Protestant brave.

Only in Maryland were there any Roman Catholics in sufficient numbers to carry weight, and here Cecil Calvert, Lord Baltimore, was so influenced by the prevailing Protestant spirit—as well as so anxious for religious tolerance—that no man was allowed to call another by a religious nickname. All through the Republic's formative period, Roman Catholics were few in numbers, negligible in influence.

Protestantism and the growth of America walked hand in hand during the Colonial days. On every frontier was the church; it was worship center, social meetinghouse and town hall, all in one. In its emphasis upon liberties, its unimpeded search for truth and its freedom from authoritarian control of all kinds, the character of the nation coming to birth was Protestant to the core.

And Protestantism has not only made the American heritage; it has again and again brought the nation back to it. When both Puritanism and patriotism waned and weakened, it was a revived Protestantism that launched the Great Awakening in the eighteenth century and strengthened the nation for the bitter test of the Revolutionary War. Such clerical cyclones as Jonathan Edwards the Congregationalist, George Whitefield the Methodist, Theodore Frelinghuysen the Dutch Reformed, and Gilbert Tennent the Presbyterian blew mighty bugles reminding Americans of their calling as spiritual freemen. The Great Awakening, say historians, cradled the rebellion.

Under the eloquent preaching of such men sat those who soon were to be called the Founding Fathers. In Episcopal pews sat Washington, Patrick Henry, John Hay, Robert Morris, John Marshall, Alexander Hamilton, George Mason, Samuel Livermore, C. C. and Charles Pinckney, James Madison, John Randolph, Richard Henry and "Light Horse Harry" Lee. In Presbyterian pews were Constitutional Convention delegates Gunning Bedford, Jr., William Paterson, William Richardson Davie, Luther Martin and William Livingston; there too were the men shortly to become Washington's leading generals: Knox, Sullivan, Stark, Mad Anthony Wayne, Morgan, Pickens.

In Congregational pews sat such members of the Constitutional Convention as Oliver Ellsworth, Abraham Baldwin, Nicholas Gilman, Elbridge Gerry, Rufus King, John Langdon and Caleb Strong; it was Congregationalist John Adams who wrote: "Statesmen may plan and speculate for Liberty, but it is Religion and Morality alone which can establish the principles upon which Freedom can securely stand. A patriot must be a religious man."

Presbyterian John Witherspoon, later to serve in the Continental Congress and to sign his name to the Declaration of Independence, the only clergyman to do so, left his post as president of the College of New Jersey (now Princeton University) to stump the country and warn that the British were coming. A towering figure, this Witherspoon. James Madison was one who

The Declaration Committee was made up of Thomas Jefferson, John Adams, Benjamin Franklin, Roger Sherman and Robert Livingston. All were deeply imbued with the Protestant vision of freedom, equality of opportunity and the right to happiness for all.

studied under him; among others who as students imbibed his love for freedom were a vice-president, ten cabinet members, sixty congressmen, twelve state governors, three Supreme Court justices.

Baptists almost to a man, clergy and laity alike, readied themselves for the coming conflict. George Washington later praised them for being "uniformly and almost unanimously the firm friend of civil liberty and the preserving promoters of our glorious Revolution."

Swedish and German Lutherans, who only a generation before had formed themselves into the Lutheran Church in America, swiftly got in on the birth of the nation. The sons of Henry Melchior Muhlenberg, American Lutherism's patriarch, were among the Revolution's firebrands. One of them, John Peter Gabriel Muhlenberg, interrupted his sermon one January Sunday in 1776 to say: "There's a time to preach and a time to fight!" and forthwith stepped out of his pulpit and into the Continental Army. It was a Lutheran who rang the Liberty Bell, Lutheran women who stitched the first American flag, designed by the devout Betsy Ross. (Continued on page 18)

TOP
Recognition of their dependence upon Almighty God for guidance in every move affecting the nation's welfare was seen in the very beginning. The first prayer in Congress, September 5, 1774, in Carpenter's Hall, Philadelphia, set the pattern—and to this day both houses of the Congress open their sessions with prayer by officially appointed chaplains.

LEFT
Washington and members of Congress attending Christ Church, Philadelphia, in 1781. An outspoken churchman, Washington's famous statement, "I shall always strive to prove a faithful and impartial patron of genuine, vital religion," was typical of government leaders of that day.

TOP

"It is impossible to reason without arriving at a Supreme Being," said Washington on many an occasion. His constant habit of seeking God's guidance, as during the threatened defeat of the Continental Army camped at Valley Forge in the winter of 1777-78, helped him turn many a potential defeat into glorious victory.

RIGHT

From the inauguration of the first President of the United States, at Federal Hall, New York City, April 30, 1789, no Chief Executive has taken office without swearing, hand on Bible, to perform his presidential obligations, "so help me, God."

The Declaration of Independence is not only one of the world's great political documents; it is also, and primarily, a religious Magna Carta —written and signed by men to whom religion was all-important as the basis of lasting freedom. Its glowing principles were written "with a firm reliance upon the protection of divine Providence." Among the fifty-six signers, none was an "unbeliever"; only one was a Roman Catholic. There were thirty-four Episcopalians, thirteen Congregationalists, six Presbyterians, one Baptist, one Quaker. Before they strode forward to append their signatures, each man bowed his head in prayer.

Modern politicians tend to treat religion cautiously—or only for political effect. These authors and signers of the Declaration spoke of God boldly, reverently. On behalf of the new nation, they said, they were assuming "the separate and equal station to which *nature's God*" entitled them. The self-evident truth they voiced was that men were *"endowed by their Creator"* with unalienable rights. They appealed to *"the Supreme Judge of the world"* for the rectitude of their intentions.

Recognizing that religion was the very cornerstone of the new nation, they were careful to give it full credit and proper place. Proper place was first place. In 1774 the Continental Congress appointed chaplains to conduct prayers for the Congress, to accompany the Revolutionary armies in the field. The Congress adopted also a position on Protestant tolerance which set the tone for our national as well as denominational regard for other men's faiths. To the inhabitants of Roman Catholic Quebec, worried about the amity of the new Protestant nation, went an official message of assurance that "the transcendent nature of Freedom elevates those united in her cause above all such low-minded infirmities" as prejudice arising from differences in religion. And a year later,

when George Washington sent Benedict Arnold into Quebec on a special mission, he devoted a large portion of his instructions to charging Arnold to "protect and support the free exercise of the religion of the country and the undisturbed enjoyment of the rights of conscience in religious matters."

That was the spirit of the Founding Fathers. That is the American spirit today. Deep and firm into this country's cornerstone went the Protestant principle of religious tolerance. And all the carping of narrow sectarians, all the sad lack of reciprocity on the part of non-Protestant nations, all the jibes by those who interpret tolerance as weakness, have never been able to chisel it out. Well might it be Protestantism speaking in Edwin Markham's lines:

> He drew a circle that shut me out—
> Heretic, rebel, a thing to flout.
> But Love and I had the wit to win:
> *We drew a circle that took him in.*

If you want further proof of the part played by "religion pure and undefiled" in the foundations of our heritage, look in at the Constitutional Convention of 1787. Here were assembled men charged with creating one of the most revolutionary documents of all time, the American Constitution. But the going was slow. For five weeks the delegates had been wrangling, arguing, sweating; they hadn't been able to agree on a single line. Then it was that Ben Franklin heaved his squat bulk out of his chair and addressed himself to a point of order. "Mr. Washington," he said, "the small progress we have made is melancholy proof of the imperfections of the human understanding. In this situation of this assembly, groping as it were in the dark to find political truth, and scarce able to distinguish it when presented to us, how has it happened, Sir, that we have not hitherto once thought of humbly applying to the

Father of Lights to illuminate our understanding. . . . I have lived, Sir, a long time; and the longer I live the more convincing proofs I see of this truth, that God governs in the affairs of man. . . . We have been assured, Sir, in the Sacred Writings, that 'except the Lord build the house, they labour in vain that build it.' I firmly believe this. . . . I therefore beg leave to move that hereafter prayers, imploring the assistance of Heaven and its blessings on our deliberations, be held in this assembly every morning before we proceed to business."

The weary delegates arose and cheered. The motion was unanimously approved and voted. Is it strange that from that moment onward progress was rapid in the framing and adoption of The Constitution of the United States?

Yet, religiously motivated at it was, the Constitution did not contain enough religion in it to suit the people. When it went out for ratification, a public clamor arose. How about freedom of religion? Certainly, it was basic in the whole new system. But the people wanted it down in black and white. And how about complete separation of Church and State? Some states still had one "authorized church," with taxation to support it, and tolerance for dissenting bodies. Others had several "established" churches, with tax income divided among them. But the move lately had been away from both "single establishment" and "multiple establishment" toward no establishment at all.

The struggle for disestablishment had been highlighted in Virginia, where the Church of

In the Great Seal of the United States, the religious aims and foundations are signified: E Pluribus Unum (Many in One) expresses the Protestant principle of unity within diversity; and a pyramid representing the incomplete nation topped with the all-seeing eye of God, carries Latin legends proclaiming that "God has favored the undertaking" and that, based firmly on religious faith, "a new order of nation was thus launched."

England was the state church. There young James Madison and Thomas Jefferson had been carrying the torch for complete separation of Church and State. The latter had written his "Bill for Religious Freedom"; the former had inscribed his famous "Memorial and Remonstrance Against Religious Assessments." Jefferson took the part of the Quakers, who had sought "these new countries as asylums of civil and religious freedom," but had found them "free only for the reigning sect." Madison pled for a tolerance that would reach out to Jews and others as well as differing Christian groups, saying: "Who does not see that the same authority which can establish Christianity, in exclusion of all other religions, may establish with the same ease any particular sect of Christian in exclusion of all other sects?"

The fever was catching; the people wanted the whole matter cleared up once and for all. They demanded a complete bill of rights.

Meanwhile, the Constitution awaited ratification; without it there was no Union. To get it ratified, Madison and others promised to work for amendments that would guarantee, for now and forever, the American citizen's rights—religious and civil.

Is it strange that religion came first? Not to the American aware of his heritage! Nor is it strange that men of deep-running Protestant convictions were responsible for this and all other freedoms being clarified.

To Madison, whose prominence in framing the Constitution and whose purity of life and faith nobody questioned, fell the task of preparing that first statement of fundamental freedoms.

On June 8, 1789, Madison brought his draft of the proposed Bill of Rights before the House of Representatives. In the prime position given the freedoms demanded in the First Amendment was Religion. The wording given the other freedoms in the same paragraph—of Speech, Press, Assembly and Petition—was quickly approved. But for three and a half months the House and Senate debated the terminology for Freedom of Religion, changing the words around, deleting, adding, clarifying. At no time in our history, and in behalf of no other measure, has so much care and attention been lavished on one sentence of legislation.

What these men of vision and faith finally came up with may not please those who, in our day, would revise our basic pattern of separation of Church and State. But there it stands: "Congress shall make no law respecting an establishment of Religion, or prohibiting the free exercise thereof." This was not government washing its hands of religion; it was government taking the deepest and broadest interest in it; it was government carefully and prophetically protecting religion by forever removing religious rights from the tampering of any public functionary, any self-seeking hierarchy. It took vision, inspired vision, to do that.

Twist those words as you will, you cannot make "separation" mean renunciation. Our national culture is permeated with religion. Witness the religious phraseology in our state as well as national constitutions; forty-three of the forty-eight are redolent of man's reliance upon God. Witness the chaplains praying their prayers before every session of Congress. Witness the religious oaths required for officeholders, the religious exercises at official ceremonies. Witness, in every court in the land, the swearing, right hand on the Bible, to "the truth, the whole truth, and nothing but the truth, *so help me God.*" Witness the tax exemptions granted religious institutions. Witness the legend "In God We Trust" on your coins, placed there by a Protestant Secretary of Treasury. Witness on your dollar bill the Great Seal, with its pyramid representing the thirteen

Protestant churches are closely identified with important events in American history. One is the Old North Church in Boston with its majestic tower and commemorative tablet: "The signal lanterns of Paul Revere displayed in the steeple of this church April 18, 1775, warned the country of the march of British troops to Lexington and Concord."

original colonies, topped by the all-seeing eye of God surrounded by a cloud of glory, symbolizing the protecting Divine Presence.

The American, be he pagan or pious, can no more escape reminders of the American Protestant heritage than he can escape his skin. He is surrounded on all sides by the fruits of the staunch Protestant insistence that this free land should express *God's* ideal of liberty —political, economic, social, religious. And if, in some burst of appreciation, he feels like singing about the America that is his, chances are that he will lift his voice in songs that not only tell of this nation's bounty and beauty but

pay tribute to the Author thereof. Virtually all of them were written by Protestants, God-inspired, freedom-inspired.

No American should forget, or be allowed to forget, with what price his freedom has been purchased. He should not be permitted to forget that the American heritage is the Protestant heritage. Nor should he, Protestant or Roman Catholic or Jew, or of no faith at all, fail to heed the warning sounded by James Russell Lowell who, when asked by Guizot: "How long do you think the American Republic will endure?" replied: *"So long as the ideas of its Founding Fathers continue to be dominant!"*

The American freedom ideal is seen at its purest and highest in Protestant worship. It is, to a degree unsurpassed by any other phase of American life, "of the people, by the people, for the people."

Here Christ is exalted as Savior of all mankind; and here all learn, at His feet, how love, kindness, brotherhood and joy may change the individual and, through doing so, change the whole world.

II

THE PROTESTANT AT WORSHIP

"Freedom of Worship" is no academic shibboleth to the American Protestant. He knows that this most fundamental of all his liberties not only sired his political and social freedom; it fosters and preserves and protects it. It symbolizes and makes meaningful the liberty of spirit and action which, to him, is more to be cherished than life itself. If, therefore, you would see American freedom at its highest and purest, focus your view for a moment on the Protestant at worship. No part of American life is more truly "of the people, by the people, for the people."

Protestant worship differs from that of other faiths in three main respects: the spirit of the worshiper, the character of the worship, and the status of its clergy.

The Protestant seeks his "church home" as a free man chooses the place he will live, the clothes he will wear, the food he will eat, the vocation he will follow. No government commands and no hierarchy dictates where he shall go. Only he and his God know the peculiar and particular requirements of his soul. In the dignity of his individuality, he chooses the church whose doctrines most nearly match his needs for spiritual sustenance, whose congregation affords him fellowship with those with tastes like

his own, whose program offers him the best place to invest his special talents and enthusiasms and interests.

He has a rich and wide variety to choose from. Does his spiritual temperament find readiest response to solid doctrine propounded amid stately ritual and dignified ceremonial? Then he will be comfortably at home with Episcopalians, Lutherans, or Presbyterians. Does he want more simplicity in ecclesiastical decor, greater liberality in doctrine, more emphasis on social duty? Then he may turn in at the wide-open doors of Congregationalists or Friends. Or is it a combination of these elements, with somewhat more emotional warmth and challenge to social action, he is after? Then he will find it with Methodists, Baptists, Disciples, Reformed, Brethren or any of several other so-called "middle-class" denominations. Does he feel the urge for more informality in worship, plus greater emphasis on fundamental doctrine and evangelical fervor? Then he may well find rapport with the Nazarenes, some Southern Baptists, the Salvation Army. Do his tastes run even more to love of revivals where the "old-fashioned Gospel" is constantly being preached to save men as "brands from the burning"? Then he will join with one of the many fervidly

(Continued on page 28)

In Protestantism the position of the clergy is unique. The minister stands among his people "as one who serves." He is a free man in a free pulp confronting free worshipers in the pews.

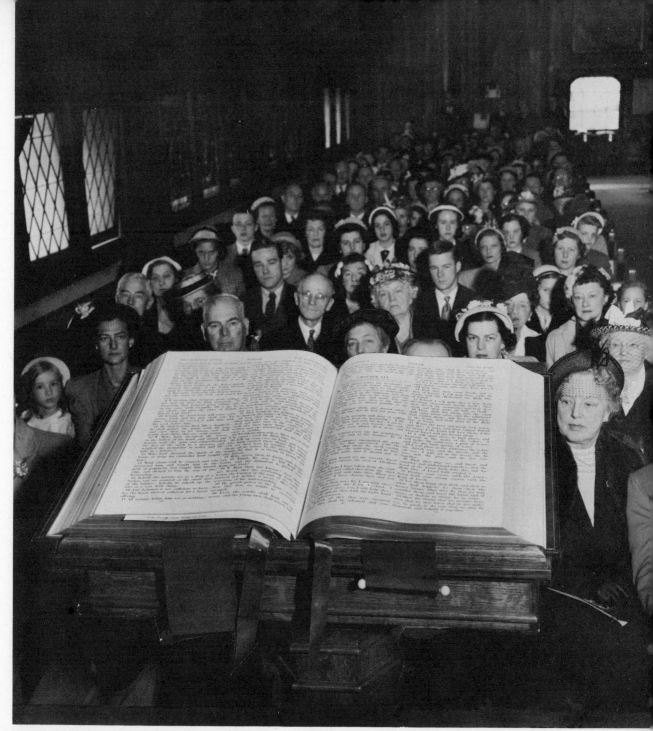

In every Protestant church the Bible occupies central place. It is an open Bible, open to all, and its precepts are interpreted out of the shared experience of the body of believers. In the solemnity of God's house, true worship evolves from the Scriptural admonition to teach the will of God through His divine Word. No Protestant service is held without a reading from the Holy Scriptures.

Music is Protestantism's unique contribution to worship. In his churches the Protestant finds his soul inspired by choral and intrumental renditions of the world's supreme music masters, most of whom were bred in Protestantism.

Protestantism is a singing religion. Lifting its united voice in the inexhaustible melodious hymns, the congregation expresses its highest aspirations and its loftiest praise to God.

evangelistic sects to whom place and order of worship mean little and the saving of souls means everything.

The diversity before him is as wide as the human heart's cravings, as varied as the soul's tastes. True freedom of worship would not have it otherwise.

The Protestant goes to his worship, whatever its character, as a *participant*—not merely as a spectator. And he goes of his own free will. Attendance at worship is not a slavish obligation, hung with hopes of reward or avoidance of punishment. It is a privilege, the privilege of the religiously free. In a very real and vital sense, the church he selects is *his* church, not the exclusive property of any ecclesiastic or group of same. He helped plan it, pay for it. In many instances, his own hands helped erect it. His voice and vote—his participation—count in its administration.

He stands in his church in the full dignity of Protestantism's challenging principle, the "priesthood of every believer." He comes to his God direct. He needs no intermediary save the Christ in whose name he prays; he need make no circumlocution via any human way station. God's word to him is: "Son of man, stand upon thy feet, and I will speak with thee."

One cannot comprehend the glory of Protestantism save as he understands this "priesthood of every believer" principle. The glory *and* the responsibility. The Protestant knows that, as a sinner, he had to accept responsibility for his sins—and had to elect, of his own free will, to take the way out. On man God in the beginning placed a terrible but glorious choice of the free man—he could say "no" to God, or he must choose to say "yes." He cannot depend upon any human go-between to arrange things. He cannot buy his way out of sin's consequence, work his way out by doing penance. Only by faith, says the Protestant, is the Christian justified. The reformation revitalization of the great "justification by faith" doctrine brought Christianity back to its main genius. And it put the Protestant where God originally puts every man, from the Garden of Eden onward: squarely on his own.

In the character, as in the place, of his worship, the Protestant again expresses his freedom. Yet it is a common character that emerges here. Whether the church of his choice be liturgical or evangelical, there is a unity of substance in Protestant worship that overreaches all differences in architecture, forms of worship, doctrinal interpretations.

For one thing, there is the centrality of the Bible. To the average Protestant, of whatever persuasion, the Word of God is the supreme authority. It is an open Bible, available to all. Its precepts are interpreted out of the shared experience of the body of believers. Each must search its truths for himself, obey its injunctions as the final arbiter. To each worshiper, guided by the revealing light of the Holy Spirit, falls the responsibility of finding in the Scriptures God's way for him. Do disagreements as to interpretation come? Certainly, and communions have been divided and churches split by such disagreements. But man himself must decide! Abhorrent to the Protestant is any suggestion that the final determination of God's Holy Word can be assumed by any fallible man or institution. *(Continued on page 33)*

In tens of thousands of churches across the land, volunteer choirs contribute their time and talents **to "making melody unto the Lord." Music is the great blender of the Protestant fellowship.**

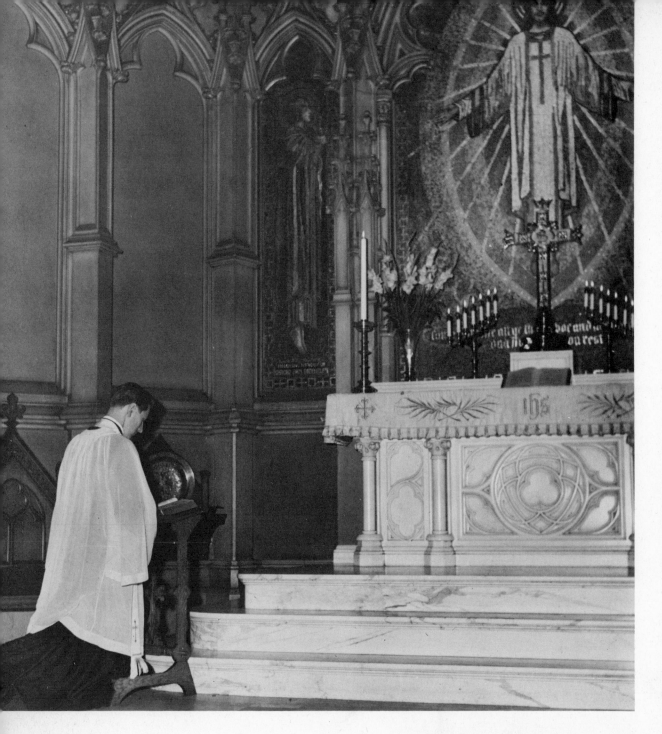

The diversity of Protestant worship includes services rich with ritual as well as simple in ceremonial. Always central, however, is the Bible and the Risen Christ.

One of the two Protestant sacraments is Holy Communion. For this, bread and wine are prepared on the Lord's Table. Before offering the elements to the communicants, prayers of invitation, confession and consecration are recited. First the bread is administered: "Take, eat; this is my body which is given for you." Then the cup is received: "This cup is the New Testament in my blood; this do as oft as ye drink it, in remembrance of me."

The only other sacrament practiced by Protestant churches is baptism, either by immersion or by sprinkling. Pools for baptism by immersion may be seen in Baptist, Disciples of Christ and Seventh-Day Adventist and several other smaller denominations which practice baptism by immersion of the whole body. Received in the baptistry by the minister at regular public worship, the candidate responds with the profession of faith in Christ as Savior and Lord. Then, as the candidate is slowly lowered into the water, the moving ceremony of symbolic rebirth is performed.

Infant as well as adult baptism is a rite practiced by some but not all Protestant denominations. In churches where this rite is observed, parents and sponsors gather with the minister before the baptismal font to dedicate the infant to the Christian life. The parents solemnly promise to teach the child to know and follow the Christian life, and to direct its youthful mind according to teachings of the Holy Scriptures. The minister takes the babe in his arms and, in the name of the Father and the Son and the Holy Ghost, baptizes it by pouring or sprinkling water on its head.

The Protestant finds unity too in the Apostles' Creed. When he squares his shoulders, lifts his eyes and affirms: "I believe in God, the Father Almighty . . . and in Jesus Christ, His only Son, our Lord," he expresses what is for him a "fundamentalism" unimproved by a hundred generations of doctrinal jugglers. When he declares: "I believe in the holy catholic Church," he is asserting his membership in the Church Universal, the mystical company of believers of all time, all places, all Christian creeds.

Symbols have more or lesser importance to the Protestant according to the traditions of his

Worship in a meeting-house of Friends bears no resemblance to public worship in any other Protestant church. Friends (Quakers) believe that worship is a personal matter between the soul and God, and can be carried on without a minister. As they sit in quiet meditation, a Friend occasionally stands to give his testimony, inspired by the "Inner Light."

At the opposite pole from the almost stark simplicity of the Quaker meeting is the colorful and stately liturgy of the high Episcopal service. To Episcopalians, some more than others, God speaks clearest and most convincingly through the stately ceremonial for which their church—and to some extent the Lutheran—is noted.

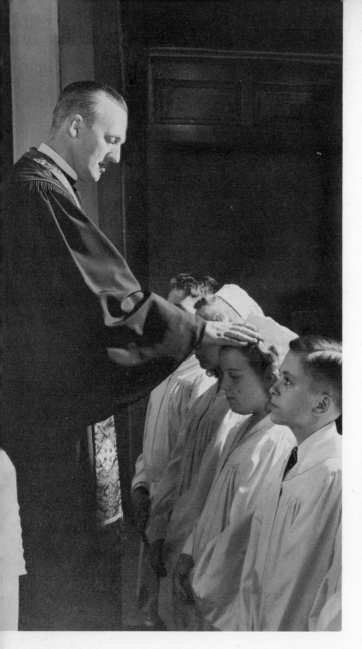

Confirmation of the young is a significant ceremony in several denominations. Preceded by a period of religious training in Christian truth, the rite admits young people into full membership of the church. Following the ceremony, the confirmants join the adults in the privilege of receiving Holy Communion.

church. One symbol, however, is basic—the cross. The Protestant cross, unlike the crucifix with its image of the dead Jesus, speaks of life and triumph, rather than death and defeat. It echoes the Master's thrilling pronouncement, "I am He that was dead; behold, I am alive for evermore!" That empty cross expresses the central doctrine of Protestantism—the Resurrection.

As to sacraments, the Protestant finds common ground with every other Protestant in his recognition of but two: Baptism and the Lord's Supper. True enough, the observance differs in different churches, but Protestants long ago ceased fighting over modes of administration and shades of meaning. The Protestant, laity and clergy alike, interprets his Lord's "Drink ye, *all,* of it" as an inclusive invitation. Holy Communion, whether "open" or "closed," whether taken at altar or in pews, is not the subject for contention it once was. Some churches still keep communion closed to all but their own members. Mostly, Protestant churches share the cup and the bread with all who will "take the cup and call upon the name of the Lord."

The great blender of the Protestant fellowship is music. Music is also Protestantism's unique contribution to worship. In his churches, the Protestant finds his soul inspired by the thrilling fugues and chorales and oratorios of the world's supreme music-masters. Is it strange that so many of the creators of immortal music were born and bred in the creative Protestant spirit? Melody bursts spontaneously from the heart made free. When the gifted mind and talent is lighted with the Gospel, great music is born.

Sunday after Sunday, in two hundred thousand and more churches throughout the land, one hears the music of Handel, who mingled his genius with devotion and gave the world such immortal works as "The Messiah." Or of Bach, who found his inspiration in Protestantism and reached his zenith with his musical interpretation of the emotional power of "justification by faith." Or of Gounod, who started out to be a preacher but turned instead into the ministry of harmonic melody that will be sung and played while time lasts. Or of Mendelssohn, whose father so implanted in the brilliant young Felix the glories of faith that these, according to the composer himself, "formed the sacred fire within me." Scores of others could be brought in as testimony, right down to Walter Damrosch, who began his musical career as a choir boy, and at twenty-two was director of music at Henry Ward Beecher's church in Brooklyn.

Protestantism's gift to music, both sacred and secular, cannot be estimated. Says James Hastings Nichols: "No other branch of Christianity in history has made such contributions to music, both directly by its development of liturgical masses, chorales and the like, and indirectly, by training the whole nation to a high level of musical taste."

And look for a moment at Protestantism's hymnody. From the time Jesus fortified the hearts of his disciples with that hymn at the Last Supper, the spirit of Christianity has been a singing spirit. "And when they had sung an hymn, they went out" has been the record ever since. Every spiritual renaissance has had its troubadours of sacred song, like Martin Luther and Charles Wesley, who have given wings to every singing revival of faith. Protestant hymns all through the centuries have inspired, comforted and aroused the spirits of generations of worshipers.

America's Protestant founders placed happy stress on hymnody, made their faith a *singing* faith. Ever since, a mighty army of poets, musicians and publishers have combined their talents to pour thousands of compositions into multiplied millions of hymnbooks. Just to mention a few: Thomas Hastings wrote a thousand tunes ("Rock of Ages") and the words of six hundred hymns. George James Webb wrote "Stand Up For Jesus" and many other sacred songs and cantatas. William Bradbury gave us, among many others, the tunes for "He Leadeth Me" and "Just As I Am." And there is Robert Lowry's "I Need Thee Every Hour," and John R. Sweeney's "Beulah Land" and "Sunshine In My Soul," and P. P. Bliss's "Hold the Fort," "Almost Persuaded" and "Let the Lower Lights Be Burning"—not to mention the more than

The reception of new members into the church is held during worship service on the Lord's Day designated for their formal admission into the congregation. Reminded of their privileges and responsibilities in seeking the Kingdom of God, the new members are called to be loyal to the church, to attend its services and support its work with love and faith. The right hand of fellowship is extended to each: "We receive you into our communion and welcome you with joy to our fellowship."

In addition to standard services for average congregations, there are within Protestantism many churches which provide worship opportunities for those with specialized needs, such as deaf-mutes who "sing" hymns with hands and not vocally. In the stillness of the sanctuary dedicated to the mute, the minister delivers his soundless sermon quite as eloquently by the deft and graceful movement of his hands as do his fellow-ministers through the employment of their vocal cords.

five thousand hymns written by blind Fanny Crosby.

Protestant music hath charms indeed. Today the presses of hundreds of denominational and independent publishing houses never cease to roll out millions of hymnbooks, organ and vocal and instrumental music. Protestantism has kept America singing the songs of faith. Estimate, if you can, what this has meant to our spiritual culture.

Consider now the unique position of the Protestant clergy. The minister is precisely that: a minister. He stands among his people as "one who serves." He is a free man in a free pulpit, confronting free worshipers in the pews. His is a specialized vocation, a high and holy calling.

But he has not separated himself from his people, nor from the common life and experiences of common men. Save for the character of his mission, he is a man among all men, tempted in all points as they are, triumphant in all points as they would like to be. In most cases, he knows by experience the bafflements and the joys of raising a family. That is good— for himself, for his people and for American life. The dedication of his character, the wholesome and challenging environment of his home life, reaches far afield. From the parsonages and manses of ministers have come a veritable army of the famous. Read *Who's Who* and see there the towering percentage of leaders in business and the professions, in science and the arts, who have been proud to record that they were "preachers' kids."

The Protestant minister has given years to preparation of heart and mind for the shepherding of his people. In America there are no fewer than two hundred seminaries, theological departments of colleges, and Bible and Christian-training institutes, where he may school himself for the ministry to which he is called. From his pulpit and out amongst his people, the Protestant minister calls forth their loyalties, articulates their inmost strivings, challenges their faith and action, "comforts the afflicted and afflicts the comfortable." His congregation loves and reveres him, follows his lead, as he welds them into a closer worshiping body.

But no Protestant minister would be so spiritually vainglorious as to claim that he, because of wearing the cloth, wears also special favor in God's eyes. Ever has it been in history that when a faith loses spiritual power, it adds snobbish pretensions, creates favored classes. The evil of this, as E. Stanley Jones has pointed out, is that "in making special classes sacred, other men have been rendered non-sacred." That does violence, not only to religion, but to the democratic principle of man's inherent dignity and importance before God.

It is Protestantism that has loosed Christianity from the bonds of specially sacred and privileged classes, and has centered that sanctity and responsibility in every true worshiper. The minister stands not one whit above the humblest layman. God's free grace has been given to all alike.

Together, all Protestants, minister and people, seek and find God in a matchless mutuality of spirit. Sunday after Sunday, and many times during the week, they come to their chosen places of worship. Some are bare and unadorned store fronts, some are plain little rural churches, some are magnificent edifices with soaring steeples reaching toward heaven. Protestantism has many great city churches; its strength, however, like the strength of America itself, is out in the small towns, the countryside, the rural areas. But whatever the sanctuary, the spirit of worship is the same.

These millions of Protestants come weary and burdened, full of the cares that infest the day, drained by the exertions and anxieties,

(Continued on page 47)

The Protestant minister, like the men of his congregation, is a family man, knowing by experience the joys and bafflements of raising and holding together a family. From the parsonages and manses of ministers have come a veritable army of the famous.

The ancient custom of divine service in the fields survives in the practice of rural congregations in praying for abundant harvests. Newly planted fields are blessed with devotion, and later in the year, when Thanksgiving is celebrated, the people lay before the altar a portion of their labor's bounty as a token of their thankfulness.

The outdoor evening worship service in the summer is popular with rural and small-town congregations. Here, as always in Protestant worship, the singing of hymns exalts the assemblage.

Itinerant preachers and revivalists tour the counties, setting up tents for services. Such meetings reach many of the unchurched, and often result in the establishment of regular congregations.

THE PROTESTANT AT WORSHIP *45*

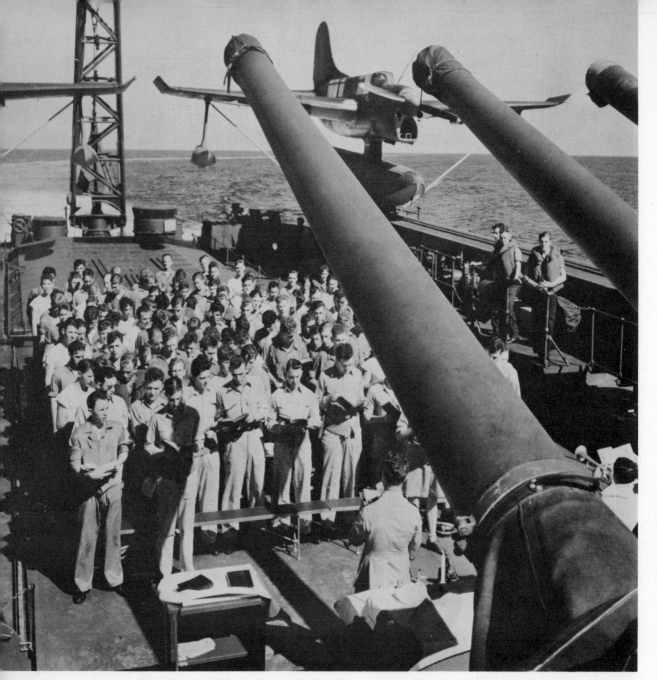

Protestantism has followed its young in the armed forces with chaplains who bring their gallant ministry to camp and shipboard, and who are especially effective with troops in combat areas. Also, the United Fellowship of Protestants, which in World War II functioned as the Service Men's Christian League, provides an effective contact between service personnel and the home churches.

the confusions and frustrations of life. They come uncoerced, and they come with open hearts to the God who speaks direct to them as individuals. They hear the Holy Word, the inspiring music, the message of their minister; they raise their voices in the inspiring hymns, bathe their souls in that communion of fellowship peculiar to the Protestant Church.

And what they see and hear and feel "makes the wounded spirit whole and calms the troubled breast, is manna to the hungry soul and to the weary rest." Their eyes, dulled with care and with looking upon human frailty, their own and others', brighten with inner light. Littleness and contention and worriment fall away. Their spines straighten, their hearts are warmed, their minds enlightened. And they go forth from their House of God whole again, free again, to face life as they must live it, to put into practice their freshened ideals, to share with their community the gifts of grace their God has vouchsafed them.

Protestantism, based on the "priesthood of all believers" doctrine, gives unique position and prominence to laymen. In co-operation with their minister, they form and perform church policy, formulate and raise the church budget, have a vote and a voice in all church matters, are committed to the inspiring principle of stewardship—with responsibility.

III

THE PROTESTANT LAYMAN

The Protestant genius is nowhere seen in such sharp focus as in the position and prominence it gives to the man in the pew. No system of faith since time began has done so much to accent and to activate the layman. Such place and power for the laity is a direct outgrowth of that basic Protestant principle, the "priesthood of every believer." It restored to Christianity its fundamental democracy, wherein there are no mysteries, positions or privileges open to the clergy which are not open also to laymen.

Look into the past history and present performance of other faiths. Where are the organic powers and prestige concentrated? In the clergy, the leaders, the mahatmas. These are the set-apart ones, on whom divine favor and privilege devolve; these are "the religious," and all other vocations are by implication unreligious.

Protestantism recognizes that Christianity was in the beginning a *lay movement*. It remembers that Jesus himself, unordained by· any earthly hierarchy or institution, despised by the priestly classes, was a layman in the strictest sense. It notes that the men He chose to spread His Gospel were drawn from secular pursuits; there was not an ecclesiastic among them. It recalls that many of early Christianity's historic happenings occurred in *lay* assemblages—as at Pentecost, where the Spirit of Truth, God's highest gift since His own Son, descended upon *lay* workers, in a home and not a church, and while nobody was leading the meeting, nobody was intervening on behalf of the others.

Centuries before Protestantism became a term, its spirit was alive in men and movements. This spirit was the genius of the Early Church, which spread the Gospel through the Roman world by "inspired amateurs"—peddlers, carpenters, sailmakers, farmers, soldiers. It proved, all down the ages, that Christianity's fastest and broadest advances could be made by men who, while operating as "ordinary citizens," glorified their calling as citizens also of the Heavenly Kingdom. Protestantism, by elevating every believer to the priesthood, has brought him off the sidelines and out of the grandstand, put him into the arena as a participant on equal par with the clergy. It has restored the spiritual dignity of man—and, as freedom always does, made him responsible.

What that imbuement of dignity and responsibility has done to the laity of Protestantism adds up to an inspiring story. Also it explains, as nothing else can explain, American democracy and its amazing achievements. Toss a torch of freedom and responsibility at a man, and you have started fires that not only warm his spirit but set him flaming—creatively, constructively—in every realm of life.

When God touches a man's personality he touches also his purse. From the Protestant laymen's purses is poured nearly a billion dollars annually to sustain their churches and promote religious activity.

It was so in the beginning. Protestant churchmen—free in mind, free in spirit—gave us the American way of life, our free enterprise, our prosperity. They wrote their faith into our political, social and scientific framework. They took religion out of the cloister and universalized it, naturalized it. They removed sanctity from the exclusive possession of any one class, any one place, and put it like a mantle on every man's shoulders, hung it like an aura over every occupation, every interest, every walk in life. They made religion more than a ritual in church, a rite in sanctuary. They brought religion down to earth and into life—*all* life. They insisted that the monk in his monastery or the minister in his pulpit was not necessarily any more holy than the merchant behind his counter, the farmer behind his plough, the businessman at his desk, the laborer at his bench. They haloed every vocation with the text: "The place *whereon thou standest* is holy ground." They faced every evil in the social order with the song, "Rise Up, O Men of God!"

In the church of his choice, the Protestant layman is a man committed to the inspiring principle of stewardship—of self and of substance. The commitment is volitional, in no sense coerced. As a voluntary "worker together with God," he pours into his church his time, his talents, his money. From infancy he has been saturated with the inspiriting truth that this church of his is just that—*his*. It is, by the grace of God, an institution "of the people, by the people, for the people."

The tasks that laymen perform in the local church are as various as the talents represented. They sit on official boards, help frame church polity, attend to legal and property matters, formulate and raise the church budget, help plan and promote the church program, usher at worship services, sing in the choir, serve as lay leaders and visitation evangelists, as church-school leaders and teachers, work together for church and community in men's brotherhood groups, foster fellowship within their own and other Christian bodies in the community.

The Protestant craves something more energetic than pew-sitting. The contribution of his time and talent is enormous in the millions of hours and million of man-power units he freely gives. In the running of his church, he has a vote and a voice. As a spiritual freeman, he uses both—vigorously.

Tasks done by laymen are as varied as their talents. Every church program enlists the help of Protestants who usually are also community leaders. One of the great occasions in the life of any church is the mortgage-burning ceremony, made possible by the tireless work of Protestant laymen who had a hand in the planning and building of the sanctuary—and in liquidating the debt.

To the Protestant his church is exactly that—his. He takes pride in its appearance as well as its program, devoting time and money to help make the House of God the most attractive place in town.

To the Protestant it is axiomatic that when God touches a man's personality, He touches also his purse. Out of the American Protestant's purse annually goes nearly a billion dollars to sustain the Christian Church program. No levies are put upon him; his is a free-will offering, not a "collection." Furthermore, he receives a strict accounting of what was done with his dedicated money. All records of receipts and expenditures are open to his investigation; church accounts are audited and reported to him; in many cases he himself is the church treasurer, or otherwise he sits in the seat of administration of funds. What that sense of money stewardship has influenced him to do in wider areas than his church, we shall see presently. What it does for his church alone is nothing short of tremendous. A billion free dollars a year, freely given!

In the larger areas of religious life and organization, your Protestant is likewise free, likewise responsible. There are few denominations whose synodical and national conclaves do not include, on an equal basis with the clergy, a representation of the laity. Whether the government of his church be Congregational, Episcopal or Presbyterian, the lay delegate makes himself heard, expresses himself without denial or duress, voices his opinions on church polity and programs. The Protestant principle of representative government is as firm at its home base as it is in the American political and social life it created.

In interdenominational affairs too, you will find laymen prominent—as delegates to official meetings, holders of important office, sparkplugs of action. They bring their trained minds and devoted hearts to every enterprise of larger Christianity. Their presence in the higher councils of the Protestant godly has sparked many of the most advanced programs of unified Christian procedure. In many of the most powerful interdenominational agencies—as, for example, the home and foreign missions and Christian education groups—you will find a veritable "Who's Who" of business and professional America—statesmen, jurists, industrialists, scientists.

Protestant lay organizations, many of them spontaneously initiated by laymen themselves, are as thick in America as trees in the forest. They form a rich pattern of spiritual vitality in special areas, and for special purposes. Many started in unexpected places, accomplish spectacular results. Protestant laymen, without benefit of clergy, founded the YMCA, the Boy Scouts of America, the Big Brother Movement, the Student Christian Movement, the Laymen's Missionary Movement, the Gideons International, and a legion of other religious and welfare movements.

Currently, one of the most significant forces in American life is the Laymen's Movement for a Christian World. This lively group sponsors Laymen's Sunday (the third in October of each year) when some 50,000 laymen take to pulpits and microphones to preach the application of Christian principles in practical affairs; taking part in 1950, for example, were such staunch Protestants as UN Chief Delegate Warren R. Austin, Senator H. Alexander Smith, Representative Walter R. Judd, Myron C. Taylor, Harold E. Stassen. Another activity of the Laymen's Movement is the conducting of labor-management conferences to apply spiritual patterns to industrial disputes. Another is the publishing and distributing of millions of handbooks and pamphlets calling for more active lay participation in church life. And on the highest levels, as well as in the humblest places, they make their potency felt. When it seemed the new United Nations was making space for everything but religion, Protestant laymen almost drowned the UN with demands for a

Breaking bread together at church suppers and social affairs affords chances for fellowship and the welding of common church and community interests. They also provide unparalleled opportunity for making the newcomer see the value of affiliation with a "church family."

For the raising of extra funds needed for special programs, most Protestant churches avoid the use of any device that resembles or leads to gambling. One favored method is the church auction.

chamber for prayer and meditation, also for a period of reverent silence at the opening of each UN Assembly wherein each delegate could commune according to his faith; they got both.

Yet another activity founded by Protestant laymen is the national, nonsectarian program, "Religion in American Life," which each November utilizes press, radio, television and display advertising to rouse the nation to the importance of religious faith. In 1950 its campaign theme was: *"Take your problems to church this week—millions leave them there!"* and in 1951: *"Take someone to church this week— you will both be richer for it."* Headed by such production geniuses as Charles E. Wilson, formerly president of General Electric and now chief of U.S. defense mobilization, and such merchant princes as James C. Penney, founder

of the department-store chain, this drive enlists some of America's top leaders.

Other centers of lay devotion are the 250 or more luncheon groups—a spiritualized Rotary or Kiwanis project—scattered across the land under the sponsorship of the Christian Business Men's Committee. What's good for lunch is also good for breakfast, and thus we have a large number of Breakfast Groups, founded by devout layman Abraham Vereide in Seattle and now directed by him from Washington, D. C., where nine groups of senators, representatives and other government leaders meet regularly to seek God's guidance in their important decisions.

Indicative too of the ever-rising importance attached to lay participation in Protestantism's high councils is the prominent place given lay-

On Layman's Sunday—the third in October—thousands of laymen take to Protestant pulpits all over the land to preach the application of Christian principles to practical affairs.

men in the new National Council of Churches of Christ in the U.S.A. Heading up the general department of United Church Men are some of America's foremost business leaders. And not only does management contribute to Protestantism's army of "inspired amateurs"; labor too has been guided by men trained in active church and community participation. Men like Walter Reuther (Lutheran), Victor Reuther (Methodist), William Green (Baptist) and John G. Ramsey (Presbyterian) developed not only their leadership skills in the local Protestant church, but fired there too their passion to help workers get a fair break in industry.

Protestantism has fed into the nation's life, at its most vital places, a veritable host of leaders in every field. One cannot begin to name them. Just pick any stage of life—industrial, scientific, medical, military, political or whatever—and you'll find the main roles glittering with names of devout men trained in the tradition of stewardship. Run your finger down any list of American great, past and present, and see there the towering totality of Protestant men.

No one need be baffled by the fact that so many of America's great creative minds in all fields have been Protestant. The unshackled mind is the only truly creative mind. Just as the Reformation struck the chains of medieval ecclesiasticism from man's spirit, so has Protestantism released the scientific and creative genius from medieval attitudes that inhibited him. Link that sense of intellectual freedom with a sense of responsibility for what happens to his fellow-man, and you have a mind and a man bound to achieve important things for God and all humankind.

As in other things, the Puritans got us off on the right foot there. They held that a man's vocation was his calling; he should regard it with the same reverence with which a minister

The essential democracy of Protestantism, which activates the principle of self-determination amid its congregations, is as available to so-called minorities as to majorities—as in Protestant work among America's original inhabitants, the Indians, who with their individuality and independence make first-class Christian laymen.

The Protestant layman's contribution of time and talent often reaches far beyond the limits of his local church. Jointly with his minister, he takes active part in denominational activities as a fully accredited and voting member of his church's conference, presbytery or synod and on educational, missionary or judicial boards.

TOP AND RIGHT

It is from the laity, deeply imbued with the equally high calling of the dedicated laymen and the ordained minister, that the Protestant clergy comes. The same impulse that led the layman to make Christian service his avocation leads him, in many cases, to make that service a vocation. From his training in seminary until his ordination, and all through his ministry, the Protestant layman-turned-minister feels that spiritual oneness with his people which is unique in the Christian clergy-laity relationship.

OPPOSITE PAGE: TOP

The United Church Canvass, locally sponsored by all Protestant churches in the community, is an effort almost entirely in the hands of energetic laymen. Such united efforts do much to make any community aware of the importance of religion—and the importance of a co-operative approach to it.

OPPOSITE PAGE: BOTTOM

Teams of lay visitors devote endless evening and Sunday afternoon hours to visiting families in the community, bringing the church and its program to newcomers and nonchurchgoers as well as to delinquent attenders and shut-ins. Such persistent lay effort is often responsible for church success.

THE PROTESTANT LAYMAN *59*

The strong democracy of Protestant church government is nowhere better seen than in the local church vestry, official board or session, where vestrymen, deacons and elders pool their experience and energy with those of the pastor to make their corner of the Kingdom effective.

regards his pulpit. So regarded, Americans soon found that prosperity generally attends the way of a man who mixes his talent with the Christian virtues of sobriety, honesty and industry. The virtues that made a good Protestant were also the virtues that made for success.

With the gaining of wealth, capitalism arose —as it must when men have any capital to deal with. American capitalism, pilloried by every pink from Moscow to Manhattan, was, in those days, nothing to sneer at. The industrious and thrifty John Calvin, father of the Presbyterian faithful, is also credited with being the father of responsible capitalism. Many of America's founders brought with them Calvin's indignant feeling about idleness and dependence. He had preached individual initiative, free enterprise, religious sanction for the profit motive. But he

had insisted that that initiative and enterprise and motive be pursued not for their own sake but for God's and humanity's. John Wesley too, with his injunction to "Gain all you can, save all you can, give all you can," gave Christians the right incentive. That was—and is—Christian capitalism. Before we jettison it, at the instance of spokesmen for foreign ideologies, we had better look around a bit at what this "stewardship of wealth" has done for us.

Americans realize that in our economic system there are plenty of inequities, plenty of wrongs that need setting right. Capitalism per se is no holy order. But Protestant laymen hold that we do ill if we forget its Christian basis in this land, and we do worse if we fail to labor ceaselessly to further Christianize it.

Protestantism lays upon all a concept of

Chosen by their fellow-laymen to represent them at denominational conclaves, laymen take their place on equal par with the clergy. The administrative and legislative power of these great assemblies vary, yet they are the supreme organs in the representative government of Protestant denominations.

money-stewardship that is unique. It teaches men not only that all wealth comes from God, but that it belongs to the society in which it was made. That concept has made of Protestant churchmen the greatest philanthropists the world has ever known. They have poured their wealth not only into their churches but also into educational, scientific and humanitarian causes beyond computation. And they have made their gifts, on the whole, without regard to creed or religion. Where else, for example, can you find such stewards as Protestants Andrew Carnegie, the Rockefellers, Andrew Mellon, Henry Ford—to name just a few? And their example has been followed, in proportion, by most Protestants according to their means.

To sum up: the Protestant doctrine of the "priesthood of every believer" has dignified the layman as has no other faith. It has imbued him with responsibility for his church, his community, his nation, his world. It has imposed upon him a stewardship of self and substance that has resulted in vast contributions to the so-called "American way of life." And it has set his feet on the highroad to human helpfulness in a manner that has made him and his country bywords for unselfish giving the like of which this needy world has never seen.

Protestant laymen, in a word, are not only the pillars of their churches; they are the stanchions of American democracy. Schooled in spiritual democracy, they have to spread that principle throughout society at large. And, it is not too much to add, they are the main hope and inspiration of democracy's spread throughout the earth.

Remarkable is the place of women in Protestant life and work. In solemn pledge services, women's groups bind themselves to dedicate their gifts and devotion to the causes embodied in many programs of church life. The women set church goals, make denominational and interdenominational commitments. Following the prayerful pledge service, they set out to work zealously for the needs they feel must be met. Active Protestant churchwomen number ten million.

IV

TEN MILLION CHURCH WOMEN

"What women these Christians have!" So exclaimed a pagan onlooker during the days of the Roman Empire. Observing the early Christian community, he had seen the women in the Gospel lead, marching beside their men with uplifted chins and shining eyes, stepping with unfaltering tread toward the lions in the Coliseum. "What women!" the pagan said.

Pagans are still saying it. Christian women are still amazing the world. They always have. Women were last at the Cross, first at the tomb. They amazed even the disciples, one of whom commented to Jesus on the Emmaus walk: "Certain women of our company made us astonished!" Likewise astonished, over and over again, are present-day churchmen who acknowledge the ladies as the prime pillars of their fellowship.

Only a fool—usually a male fool—ever apologizes for the preponderance of female influence and representation in Protestant church life. Its millions of energetic, ingenious and devoted women are the flower of this faith. It is Protestantism's peculiar glory that woman has been able to achieve her first liberty within its precincts, her fullest liberty in response to its ethic. Where else has woman found so great an outlet for her urges to self-expression? Where else has she been so challenged to effective service for her community and her world? Where else has she been taught the full powers of her leadership talents and given a chance to exert them?

What Protestant woman has done with her capacities for indignation at oppression, her sympathy with weakness, her eagerness to serve, adds up to a compelling total in American life and culture. She has sensitized the conscience of mankind, left the prints of her heels on every path toward the better life, the higher civilization. *Cherchez la femme?* That's easy. Survey your church, your community, your nation. Look closely into any lively reform, any salient advance toward the more abundant life. There, everywhere, you will "find the woman."

The modern Christian world owes a great deal to its women; the Christian woman owes a great deal more to her faith. To Christianity she owes the sanctity of her position as wife and mother, the chivalry accorded her, the protection given her in holy ordinance and civic law from masculine whim and lust, the equality and dignity she enjoys. Christianity removed the chains that immemorially had bound her; *Protestant* Christianity lifted her to her feet and set her on the long march toward full emancipation.

Does the modern woman doubt what it was that set her free? Then let her remember what

The Protestant churchwoman's first duty to her God and her church is her family. The stress placed by Protestantism on strong family life is reflected in the seriousness with which she takes her motherhood. Her children she trains, by precept and example, in Christian virtues; her home she makes a center of friendship and good neighborliness.

it was like to be a woman in pre-Christian times, or let her ponder the status of the Moslem woman today. Let her read Greek and Latin literature; she need go back no farther than the Roman era. Her rights then were scarcely on a par with those of a household pet. Society, dominated by the lordly male, held her in contempt. At best, she was a plaything; on the average, a drudge; most of the time, a slave, a chattel, a bit of man's baggage. She married to become a man's property, body and soul—bought, sold or exchanged at her master's whim. As a mother, her position was almost as degrading; she had no voice in the training of her children; legally they were not hers but her husband's.

History is filled with woman's shame. In man's world, vice and lust and immorality ruled—with woman always the victim. Even the religions of the ages did little to reduce the foolish assumptions of male superiority. In every land and clime, man monopolized religion as he monopolized everything else. Hinduism and Buddhism held—and still hold—that a woman as such cannot be saved; she must first be reborn as a man. Every day the pious Pharisee in Christ's time recited his thanks to God that he was not "a woman, a leper, or a Gentile."

Then came Jesus. With Him there was no patronizing of woman, no loud talk about woman's rights; He simply granted those rights. His attitude and words struck off the ancient chains of womanhood once and for all. Woman no longer was man's inferior; the "Gentle Man of Nazareth" gave her equal stature, equal privileges, a chance at equal powers and position. He sanctified the home, woman's chief sphere. He ennobled marriage, her main career. He glorified virtue, her finest adornment.

She began immediately to rise. It has been a long climb, with many setbacks. But through

TOP

Presiding over church meetings and making stimulating speeches in behalf of good causes is the common experience of Protestant churchwomen. As leaders of parent-children groups, as directors of religious education and teachers of religion—and in some cases as deaconesses and elders—they are pillars of church strength in any local communion.

RIGHT

In no role are the Protestant churchwomen more effective than as teachers in the church school. American women who regularly devote their talent for understanding and guiding young lives number in the hundreds of thousands.

The willing hands of faithful and energetic Protestant women engage in manifold tasks which contribute to the efficiency as well as the spirituality of their churches. Getting out mailings to the membership and making salable items for church sales are but two of hundreds of services performed by ladies' aid and other societies.

Women's choral and musical groups provide an outlet for the gifted as well as a chance for self-expression, also lift the level of congregational hymn-singing. And from church sewing circles there have flowed through the years and across the world an untold quantity of garments and other necessities for those in need.

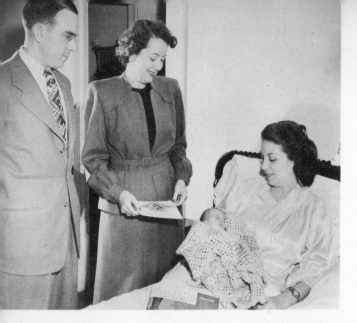

Prompt to welcome another young Protestant into the spiritual fellowship of the Cradle Roll, visitors from women's groups quickly make young parents feel the church's interest.

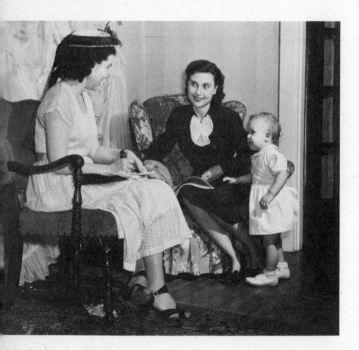

To the visitors' committee of the women's society in many a Protestant fellowship belongs much of the credit for enlisting prospective new members of church and Sunday school.

the years and the places where free Christianity has gone, woman has come up—far up. The change in her status and station has been more revolutionary than that of any segment or class, in any field of life. Nowhere has she come farther than in Protestant America.

Today the American woman takes her rights and privileges for granted; she forgets too quickly the degrading pit from which she was digged—and who and what did the digging.

The full realization of the American woman's liberty has been largely wrought for her by a host of embattled ladies. Almost without exception, those great American women who fought and won woman's emancipation were devout Christians, who found in their Protestantism the instincts for freedom and the means to wage their long war to obtain it. Woman's battle for emancipation was not won in a day or a decade or a century. It is not fully won yet. But nowhere did it get so auspicious a start as in early America.

The Pilgrim woman was a new breed. Along with her man, she stepped onto these free shores with liberty shining in her eyes. And like her man, once she had accepted the seed of liberty in her heart, the full flower was inevitable. Equally responsible was she for making the American dream come true. From the privations of the pioneer days she built a home, raised a family, with her bare hands helped establish a frontier. It was not long until she realized that in the liberty she was nurturing there was a potential for her sex greater than any realized by any other woman on earth. At home, in church, in the community, she began to assert herself.

Patroness of the American woman's freedom was Anne Hutchinson. Gallant Anne! In the Massachusetts Bay Colony she dared assert that the Puritan preachers (male) had no exclusive right to divine inspiration and revelation. She was, like Roger Williams, expelled from the colony. But it took more than expulsion to stop the crusading Anne. Only the arrows and tomahawks of the Indians on Long Island Sound could bring down this stormy petrel for woman's rights. A few smug males, back in the Massachusetts Colony, referred to her demise in 1643 as "a manifestation of divine providence." But they misread the intent of providence, underestimated the power of a woman awakened to the rights and powers of her sex.

An army of swishing skirts followed in Anne Hutchinson's train. Women began to take their place, despite all opposition, in the councils as well as the congregations of their churches. First to grant women a fuller share in religious matters were the Quakers. They not only made them elders but preachers on an equal basis with men. Rebecca Jones, Lucretia Mott, Hannah Barnard were three of many.

Methodism too had its great women. Susanna Wesley, mother of John and Charles, mothered also the tradition of Methodism's great Woman's Society for Christian Service—which in turn inspired a host of other churches' programs for the enlisting of women's graces and talents. It was a woman indeed, Barbara Heck, who is credited with founding the first Methodist Church in this hemisphere.

The Disciples of Christ had in the beginning, as now, a cordon of able women preachers. Abigail Hoag Roberts is a good example. She preached from 1814 to 1841, was often threatened with tar and feathers—sometimes by her own sex. But she drew the people in droves, as many as twelve hundred on a Sunday. When a male minister, nettled at such able feminine competition, demanded why she did not "go to the heathen" with her alleged call to preach, Abigail looked him up and down and replied: "So far as I can judge, I am in the midst of them!"

By fostering friendship and good will between different races and creeds, Protestant women have struck effective blows for tolerance, good citizenship and improved community relations.

The teaching of home economics can be made a holy exercise when such subjects as breadmaking and child-nursing is given prospective brides by voluntary church workers.

"World Community Day," one UCW project, summons Protestants each year to search closets, drawers and attics for usable articles needed by the distressed peoples of Europe and Asia.

Other ladies did "go to the heathen." Among the American Indians and across the seas went a flood of dedicated Methodist and Baptist, Presbyterian and Congregational women during the early mission expansion of the nineteenth century. A good sample was Narcissus Whitman; wife of a medical missionary, she was the first white woman to cross the Rockies to enter the great Northwest. Women were considered too frail, too modest for public life, but few hands were raised to stop them from taking on the hazards of missionary life. They promptly proved their mettle.

The ladies have not yet won complete equality as ministers. The reason probably is that not enough of them want it. Let the hankering arise on a wide enough scale, and you can put it down that universal ordination will be theirs.

Read their achievements in fields they *have* coveted. Even in Colonial times, for all the apparent hobbles placed on her, the "career girl" was in evidence. There were lady physicians and pharmacists, hotelkeepers and printers, teachers and lecturers. The "she merchant" was a recognized figure; 10 per cent of the shops were managed by women—not only dry goods, millinery and bakery, but also grocery, hardware and such.

They found an early welcome in the realm of letters. The "inky-fingered sisterhood" soon included many women earning their living by writing. Magazines began to appear in 1741 and served as an outlet for the literary urges of a host of female contributors, many of whom were in time listed among America's top literati.

Women were soon betaking themselves into many other things besides vocations. Protestant churches were beginning to pour into American life a host of women who were disturbed about things—social evils, civic reforms, woman suffrage.

Early in its rise, women quickly saw the threatening growth and the gross evil of slavery. By 1832 many of the Abolition leaders were Protestant churchwomen. On this and other evils they had long applied the cutting edge to the long and bitter fight for woman's right to suffrage. Susan B. Anthony, a flame of a woman who had organized the first woman's state temperance society in America, in 1854 began pouring her exhaustless energies into getting the vote. She started a paper, put on the masthead: "The true republic—men, their rights and nothing more; women, their rights and nothing less!" Editor of the paper was

United Church Women, a general department of the National Council of Churches, has often demonstrated its power, through use of the mails and other means, to crystallize public opinion and mobilize action for causes important to faith and world peace. It seeks to bind its members across lines of denomination, nationality and race. Making no attempt to supersede the sectarian groupings, it aims only to supplement them and to give Protestant women a strong, united voice.

Elizabeth Cady Stanton, author of a famous "Woman's Bill of Rights," who in 1854 faced New York State legislators and demanded to know "by what authority you have disfranchised one-half of the people of this state; show us your credentials that prove your exclusive right to govern not only yourselves but us!" A third member of the triumvirate of women mainly responsible for mothering woman's suffrage was Lucretia Mott, superb Quaker and superb torchbearer. This trio was followed by a succession of other great churchwomen: Frances Willard, Anna Howard Shaw, Carrie Chapman Catt, the Reverend Olympia Brown, Mrs. Oliver H. P. Belmont and a host of others.

The long battle for the franchise comprised a great and exciting era, filled with great and exciting Protestant women. It was an era in which women by the thousands found their tongues— and used them. Though not until 1920 was their victory finally won, it is to such women that belongs the credit for the 19th Amendment: *"The right of citizens of the United States to vote shall not be denied or abridged by the U.S. or by any state on account of sex."* Today's woman needs to remember that!

"The World Day of Prayer," sponsored annually by the million-strong United Church Women organization, puts Christian women of ninety-two countries on their knees together the first Friday in Lent. The UCW has instituted with striking affect a number of special-observance days.

Out of such labors has come woman's right to hold the most exalted offices in the land. Since 1920 there have been scores of women mayors of cities, governors of states, members of the U.S. Senate and House, and in 1942 there was a woman in the national cabinet. No legal reason exists to prevent a woman even being President, or Vice-President, of the United States.

Today the Protestant churches are feeding American life as never before with gifted and dedicated women. Not all or even a tithe of them take their places on the grand stage of public attention. The great majority do their important part on the home front, behind the scenes, in the little local church, the small community. But operating singly as mothers and Sunday-school teachers and faithful workers, as well as collectively in ladies' aid societies or women's leagues, they are the glory of Protestantism. On the national as well as local level of every denomination, you will find women functioning actively, energetically, creatively, on all kinds of boards and commissions, on equal status with men members.

But if you want to see woman at her most

effective, uncluttered best, you need to see her en masse in the national and regional groups for women only. Each denomination has such, and they are a mighty force. The wide field of their service reaches into the sponsorship of church schools, the maintenance of hospitals, nurseries, orphanages, homes for the aged, mission stations and projects. They exert an enormous influence, have a completely world-wide reach.

How many American Protestant women are engaged in such fervid activity on behalf of church and community? No fewer than ten million. That's right, we said ten *million!*

America's most representative women's organization today is the United Church Women, now a general department of the new National Council of the Churches of Christ in the United States of America. Its declared purpose: "To unite church women in their allegiance to their Lord and Saviour, Jesus Christ, through a program looking to their integration in the total life and work of the church and to the building of a world Christian community."

An interdenominational fellowship for action, the UCW seeks to bind its members together across lines of denomination, nationality and race. Making no attempt to supersede the sectarian groupings, it aims only to supplement them and to give Protestant women a united voice. It is made up of 1,827 local and state councils, who plan and develop their own projects but who approach them through the common motto: "Prayer, study, action."

The General Department of United Church Women has instituted with striking effect a number of special-observance days, each with a special meaning and purpose. The "World Day of Prayer" puts Christian women of ninety-two countries on their knees together the first Friday in Lent. "May Fellowship Day," the first Friday in May, directs attention to the building of Christian fraternity in homes, churches, communities, the nation. "World Community Day," on the first Friday in November, is a time for exploration of every means for achieving a peaceful world through friendly social, racial and national relations that leap all barriers. Every year the UCW conducts great nation-wide drives for clothing and food for the needy in Europe and Asia.

Make no mistake about it, the councils of churchwomen—local, state, national and international—are a potent force. They are a voice, a listening post, a dynamo. From them have come most of the leaders of the 15,000 non-church groups which today form the General Federation of Women's Clubs in America. The free Protestant woman, long trained in the tradition of activism in church, is a natural candidate for leadership in any society dedicated to correcting evils and working for the implementation of a better and more wholesome life for all.

American woman, due to her background and religious tradition, has made great strides. The oppressed, hobbled, and harnessed women of the rest of the world have seen in American woman's freedom what womanhood can and should be like. And today, in spite of tradition and opposition, they are tinkering with their chains—Mohammedan and Turkish and Hindu and Chinese. Some have them half off; others will take longer. But such is the temper toward womanhood created by the Christian society that nothing, eventually, will keep woman from coming into her own.

Protestantism's youth is its brightest and best hope. Dedicated, liberated, made responsible by Protestant precepts and opportunity for service to God and man, youth finds in the church its great-est challenge to courage, vision and meaningful action for Christ and the saving of society. Protestantism's program for the young reaches from the cradle to maturity.

V

"YOUNG AMERICA" AT ITS BEST

Christianity began with the discovery of a Child. A star of infinite brightness and infinite destiny led the Wise Men to "the place where the Child lay." That set the precedent. It seems that God has been trying for ages to tell men that where the child is, there is destiny. The wise among them have seen the light and followed it—to the child. Jesus called little children to Him, excoriated those who would forbid their coming; made Himself the Friend of youth. In its early years, the movement He began was fundamentally a youth movement—the Founder of it young, the personnel of it young, the flame of it young.

Today Christians are aware, as they have never before been aware, that tomorrow's future depends largely upon how quickly we can get to youth. For other forces too have awakened to the importance of the child. Sinister systems abroad and at home are making a terrific race for the heart and mind of the young. Christianity's race to the cradle is still on, more intense than ever.

You can chalk up Protestantism as a runner of outstanding speed and competency in the race for youth's soul. It got off to an early start. The Reformation was both launched and sustained by young men. It was youth's courage and vision that dared to challenge an ecclesiastical system grown decrepit and decaying. It was

youth's flame and imagination that dared to break with the secure and the traditional to start anew in the New World. And, on the American continent, it was these vigorous young Protestants who nailed down freedom for us all.

Today you will find no other faith that gives such prominence and position to youth. Only a free society, only a free religion, can stand against the onslaught of youth's impatience with dead tradition, its readiness to break with the past where the past is sterile, its willingness to sacrifice in pursuit of a great ideal. It is Protestant youth—dedicated, liberated, made responsible—that has kept this faith young and virile.

Protestantism's program for its youth reaches from cradle to maturity. In home and church, in community and on campus, thousands of highly trained and highly devoted specialists operate an intricate and complicated machine for the making of Christian character. That machine may have its loose bolts and screws here and there, but for decades it has been turning out the very cream of American religious, social and civic leadership. Turn where you will, you find Americans who freely assert that it was the foundation they received in some Protestant church's Sunday school or youth fellowship which gave them their start.

Robert Raikes, a layman in Gloucester, England, generally gets credit for starting the

Sunday-school movement in 1780. But a full century before Raikes rounded up his tattered roughnecks, colonists in New England were organizing and operating Bible schools for their boys and girls. Most of the initiators, like Raikes, were laymen; the clergy for a while regarded the schools suspiciously, some of them downright sniffishly. But a layman with a great idea is a hard man to stop. The Sunday-school movement in America spread, crossing denominational boundaries, bringing together local and regional church workers into a practical brand of interchurch co-operation that antedated all the "unity" projects and proposals so familiar to us today.

Sunday-school associations came into being in New York and Boston in 1816, in Philadelphia in 1817. Out of these grew the American Sunday School Union in 1824. Laymen poured their time and money into the project, expanding it later into the International Sunday School Association. Soon churches everywhere had Sunday schools. They attracted and held multitudes of children and young people. Their teaching techniques may have fallen shy of modern pedagogical standards, but they made God real, introduced pupils to Jesus Christ, illuminated positive as well as negative aspects of right and wrong, made the church important to the younger generation.

Not until the early 1900's did the denominations officially begin to take this lay-sponsored movement seriously. Then in 1910 they organized the Sunday School Council of Evangelical Denominations, which twelve years later merged with the International Sunday School Association to form the International Council of Religious Education. From then on religious education began to make strides—with the bigger denominations keeping in step and not marching each to its own music, as before.

Now merged in the National Council of the Churches of Christ in the U.S.A. as that group's education arm, the International Council during its twenty-eight years of independent life became one of the most impressive of all the big-time movements in Protestant co-operation. It brought into effective teamwork the Protestant churches' greatest educators, moved forever away from hit-or-miss Bible study toward uniform lessons, graded materials, a comprehensive curriculum. It began to tie in the home with the church as complementary media in the child's religious education, to make available elaborate courses of leadership training, to sponsor "learning by doing" projects for scholars and teachers, to impart to children a real worship experience, to encourage not mere memory work in the Bible but the understanding of great Christian beliefs, to provide actual activity in social usefulness.

The International Council of Religious Education has included forty denominations, is largest of all the various denominational groupings, and has proved itself acceptable to most conservative as well as liberal churches. Southern Baptists have their own highly efficient Sunday School Board, which provides its five million scholars and teachers with a galaxy of beautifully printed periodicals and aids to Bible study, all carefully graded, all evangelistic in tone. For those smaller denominations and independents, whose passion is to keep the Sunday school strictly Bible-centered, there is the National Sunday School Association. This association, made up of many of the same churches which co-operate with the National Association of Evangelicals, places its heaviest emphasis on revivalism, sees the Sunday school as an indispensable adjunct thereof.

Neither Robert Raikes nor those earlier sponsors of Bible schools in the colonies would recognize their baby today. But they would be vastly impressed if they could see the modern church school in action, with its trained staff and teachers, its attractive lesson materials and story papers, its audio-visual aids and television, its use of drama and pageantry, its own hymnals and children's choirs—all taking place, in many instances, in buildings or rooms or little chapels especially designed and equipped for the job being done.

It is a far cry indeed from Protestantism's early beginnings in religious education, whether you trace them to Raikes and his "ragged school" or to the rough benches of a frontier log cabin whereon sat a few pupils at one end and a devoted pioneer teacher at the other, with only a Bible between them. Today Sunday-school activity and enrollment is at an all-time high.

In 1950 Protestant church bodies reported 243,000 church schools in the United States, with a total enrollment of nearly 28,000,000 pupils and more than 2,000,000 officers and teachers.

The Sunday church school, however, is only part of Protestantism's provision for its youth. There are the vacation church schools—62,161 of them in 1949, enrolling better than 4,500,000 youngsters—which aim to occupy the idle summer hours of church children as well as to bring into the church large numbers of those who normally never darken the doors of Sunday school. There are also thousands of day camps and nursery schools, church camps and summer conferences conducted by denominations and by interdenominational groups, boys' and girls' clubs, church troops of Boy and Girl Scouts, Campfire Girls, 4-H Clubs, work-night projects and service groups which learn the meaning of social action by doing something constructive for neighborhood or town. Protestant youth is busy indeed—and busy at things that build character!

The growth and development of youth fel-

(Continued on page 82)

The Protestant church school takes children at an early age, and through a carefully graded and intelligently formulated curriculum implants in them their first understanding of such Christian virtues as prayer, love and gratitude. Lofty ideals, taught by words spoken and sung, make real to children the Christ who came to bring beauty and harmony —as well as salvation—to all His "little ones."

The pictorial presentation of Bible events and the re-enactment of life and customs of biblical days acquaint Sunday-school pupils with the great stories of the New and Old Testaments. Appealing to the child through the "eye-gate" and through activity teaching, skilled teachers are able to inculcate in interesting and adventurous fashion lasting lessons from the lives of great Bible characters.

What the children do remains their deepest experience. By active participation they identify themselves with religious teachings and practices—as when they are encouraged to offer their toys and share their pennies in simple religious services. To study the Bible efficiently is a challenging task. Maps of ancient Palestine, where Christ walked and talked, help make the Scriptures real.

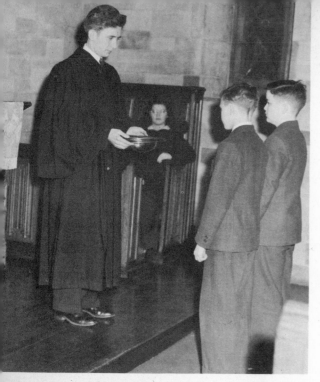

Youth conferences are conducted by all Protestant denominations during the summer months. Here group study and worship experiences leave memorable impressions on young minds.

OPPOSITE PAGE

Gradually, as they grow in stature and wisdom, Protestant young people learn how to conduct religious services for worshipers of their own age. In a devout atmosphere, they go reverently through the stages of devotional experience, singing hymns, reciting prayers together, taking the offering—and preaching the sermon. The establishment of special chapels or worship centers for children only, where they can "be themselves" without adult interference or embarrassment, is a growing practice among Protestant church planners. To children in rural regions, who by circumstances are deprived of permanent church facilities, trailer chapels bring the administration of religious education. Such emergency methods of religious instruction lack nothing of modern aids to teaching; denominations using this plan of outreach provide the latest in religious movies and visual aids. Trailer evangelism scatters the first seeds in the souls of youth, frequently leading to enrollment in church schools by mail—and eventually to established Sunday schools and church.

Thrilling climax to any period of Protestant camp life is the candlelight service which, with its meaningful ceremony conducted in the foreground of **a blazing cross on the hillside, frequently results in serious decisions made for life service, as a follower of Christ, eternal Friend of youth.**

lowships in Protestantism is something to crow about. Forerunner of them all was Christian Endeavor, founded in 1881 by Dr. Francis E. Clark. Christian Endeavor, like the Sunday-school unions, hurdled denominational boundaries as though they were not there, taught the churches their first lessons in what we now call "ecumenicity." The fervor of the Endeavorers imparted to Protestant youth a quality never matched in the modern world. Their conventions sent tens of thousands of boys and girls marching and singing through the streets. In thousands of communities, large and small, Endeavorers provided a witness to Christian unity long before many churches had seen its beauty and possibility. They were the wave of the future. Even today, after many denominations have developed their own youth fellowships, Christian Endeavor is still three million strong, with more than 80,000 societies in a hundred nations and islands of the sea.

The denominational youth groups were largely weaned on CE's flaming success. The

Methodist Epworth League, the Baptist Young People's Union (now the Baptist Training Union), the Luther and Walther Leagues and a score of others sprang up to enlist the zeal of youth in the various churches. By 1936 many of them began taking new names, calling themselves "youth fellowships," usually affixing the name of the denomination or some word related to their history.

If you would see Young America at its best, drop in at any youth fellowship assembly, in any church. Here you will find teen-agers bursting with energy, eager to know what churchmanship is all about, impatient to put religion to the test in home and school and community. They have come to discuss their problems, to ask questions, with no evasions permitted. Whether the matters agitating their young minds be theology or sex, racial differences or war, they expect a candid confronting of the problems—and get it. For Protestantism places no gag on its youth, refuses to meet honest inquiry with stuffy directives to shut up, believe

The program includes provision for fun and fellowship, but behind it is the serious purpose of orienting youth to the obligations of Christian living. This is accomplished by leadership and Bible training, through work projects in needy areas—and by many a strenuous "bull session."

what you're told, and don't question things on which the church has spoken pontifically and finally. It is the business of Protestant youth to be informed, for only the informed can be free, intelligently free, responsibly free.

The manner in which youth from these fellowships engage their interests and employ their talents for Christ is exceedingly varied. Their projects range all the way from conducting devotional and discussion meetings to staging Bible-reading programs, youth evangelism week ends, church-loyalty crusades. They sponsor National Youth Week, support missions, engage in summer work-camp activities, conduct overseas caravans, deploy themselves off to foreign lands to do relief and reconstruction. All these are fresh and dynamic expressions of the evangelistic and missionary spirit of the Christian gospel—of tremendous value for the church, of even greater value to the youth involved.

For youth particularly, fellowship is a word with broader connotations than any one com-

munion can contain. Thus, the denominational fellowships began reaching out to other groups. Their reaching, together with that of many other Christian youth agencies, brought about the United Christian Youth Movement. In recent years the UCYM has given signs of developing a good deal of the ecumenical come-on of the early Christian Endeavor. It includes within its orbit a host of denominational and independent youth organizations. In November, 1950, the United Christian Youth Movement became an affiliate of the National Council of the Churches of Christ in the U.S.A.

A spiritual phenomenon of the last decade has been the growth of Youth For Christ. Scarcely ten years old, its rise in America was spontaneous and combustious, a lively expression of the desire of American youth—mostly of the more revivalistic denominations—to witness in a large way to the Gospel's attraction for teen-agers. Now spread to a number of countries abroad, Youth For Christ centers in the United States number more than one thousand; it is an im-

Youth missions and vacation Bible schools, aimed at bringing religious education, recreation and social service to children are an important part of the Protestant outreach. Such programs are often interracial and interdenominational in approach.

pressive demonstration of unity, the more so since it brings into its fellowship some groups not especially notable hitherto for united cooperation.

Protestantism's concern for its youth extends not alone to church and community and campus. It follows its sons and daughters even to the war fronts, with chaplains, service centers, literature. During World War II occurred one of the finest examples of interchurch cooperation in Protestantism's history. It was the Service Men's Christian League, a united program designed to re-create on shipboard, in camp, and right at the fighting fronts, the youth fellowships of the churches. In the League, denominationalism was forgotten and young men and women of all communions worshiped together, planned together, maintained together the Christian approach to their sore problems of life and death. With the rise of the Korean conflict and the consequent expansion of the armed forces, the League has been revived under a new name: the United Fellowship of Protestants.

Protestant churches have done much for their youth. Youth has done much for Protestantism. It has kept the faith vibrant in vision, positive in program. It has forced always to the forefront the idea that religion's main job is not to stop something, but to start it. It has helped hold Protestantism on the beam, away from the negative, the trivial, the inconsequential. There is nothing about Protestant youth that is anti-life; it wants no truck with religion aimed only at getting people into heaven. It wants to bring heaven down to earth.

In fields of social action, Protestant young people have set a fast pace for their elders. They have taken the lead often in areas and situations of social tension, plunging forward where their elders have been slow to tread. Better even than their elders, they realize that America is deep today in a war not of political ideologies, not of economic systems, but of

Protestant churches, realizing that college years are among the most important in life, follow their youth to the campus with programs and personnel geared to the developing minds of youth who, by Protestant tradition, have been taught to think for themselves, reason for themselves—and "love the Lord thy God with all thy . . . mind." In both church and public institutions are provided worship services, counseling, discussions, fellowship and, where needed, scholarship aid. In addition there are the programs of the Student Christian and United Christian Youth Movements.

Both Protestant-founded and largely Protestant-attended, the YMCA and YWCA have contributed mightily to the spiritual and physical stature of American youth. An intelligent blend of programs aimed at developing mind, body and soul, and supervised by trained Protestant laymen, are provided for boys and girls of tender years as well as for those reaching maturity and needing guidance.

Some Protestant denominations are pioneering in the experiment of bringing to church-college campuses and summer youth assemblies students from many lands and cultures. In most Protestant church-related colleges, work opportunities are provided for the student needing self-help. An education thus gained is often more appreciated than one without this aid to the independent spirit.

The birth and growth of Youth for Christ during the past decade is one of the religious phenomena of the times. Continuing unabated in America, and now spread to a number of countries abroad, this expression of youth's response to the opportunity to witness for Christ is an indication of the evangelical Gospel's attraction for teen-agers, as well as a creator of interdenominational unity.

faiths. That war, they know, will be won by that people whose faith is strongest. Protestant youth, more serious-minded than any youth of any age, and believing more strongly in their God and their country and themselves, are out to win on every front.

Oldsters may despair these days; youngsters never. Oldsters may bewail this present world as a mess to mourn; youngsters see it as a world to wallop. Oldsters may bring in an atomic age, fumble themselves into conflagra-tion and near-cataclysm. But Christian youth, with a sense of freedom and responsibility rare if not totally absent in any other faith, have seen the atomic age come rushing in and are rushing forth to meet it—prayerfully, hero-ically, head-on. They are the people on whom our future depends.

Of the first-century Christians it was said: "They held their world together." The same may be said one day of contemporary Protestant youth!

No youth organization has meant more to the life of the religious world than Christian Endeavor. Despite the rapid recent growth of denominational youth fellowships which were largely weaned on its success, Christian Endeavor is three million strong, with more than 80,000 societies in a hundred nations and islands of the sea. Founded in 1881, it taught Protestant churches in America and abroad their first lessons in ecumenicity.

This Nation Under God

Denominational diversity is the strength of American Protestantism, part and parcel of the patterns and processes of democracy. Yet along with the preservation of this diversity, planned by the Founding Fathers from the beginning, is the steady growth of unity and co-operation between church bodies. Most significant of recent unity movements was the formation in December 1950 of the National Council of the Churches of Christ in the U. S. A. Seen above is the covenant-signing ceremony which brought the Council into being, representative of 31,000,000 members of 29 major Protestant and Eastern Orthodox denominations, pledging themselves to "exalt the Christ who recognized no barriers of sectarian differences."

VI

UNITY WITHIN DIVERSITY

The United States today, with its more than fifty million Protestants,* is the largest and most virile Protestant nation on the face of the globe. Ever since the Pilgrims reached these shores, men in search of religious liberty have been pouring into this free land, each fiercely determined to find sanctuary for his right to believe and worship as he saw fit, and as God seemed to lead. Into the savory and nourishing mixture that is American Protestantism has gone an infinitely heterogeneous assortment of individuals and groups from a rich variety of cultures in Europe and other parts of the world. One thing only they had in common: their thirst for religious liberty. If America is a "melting pot" for diverse social and political groups, it is even more of a melting pot of denominational diversity.

---

* Based on 1950 statistics gathered by *Christian Herald* from 221 Protestant denominations, this figure represents adults only. Unlike the Roman Church's accounting (28,470,092 as of January, 1951), which includes all baptized persons from infants up, most Protestant churches define as "members" only those thirteen years and older. Moreover, Protestant membership gains consistently have been larger than those of any other faith in America, both in bulk and in proportion to total strength. Few have been the years when Protestant growth has not been at least abreast of the nation's population increase; mostly it has gone beyond it—as in 1950 when Protestant churches racked up a net gain of almost 3 per cent during the same period that the population arose 1.67 per cent.

That diversity, so far from being something to carp at, is Protestantism's glory. Only he who does not comprehend the patterns and processes of democracy can fail to understand and appreciate our profusion of sects. It conforms to the rich pattern of heterogeneity that characterizes so much of life in these United States. Americans glory in their system of economic "free enterprise"; American Protestants glory too in the spiritual free enterprise that is as much a part of the American idea as States' rights and individual initiative.

Denominational diversity did not just happen. It was planned that way by the Founding Fathers. At the time of the signing of the Declaration of Independence, there were already seventeen Christian denominations flourishing in the United States, though four out of every five religionists were members of five denominations: Congregational, Presbyterian, Baptist, Episcopal and Quaker. Less than one per cent of the total population was Roman Catholic.

Did the Founders look aghast at this religious coat of many colors? They did not. They helped design it. James Madison's principle, unanimously endorsed by his compatriots, that "all men are equally entitled to the free exercise of religion, according to the dictates of conscience" started us on our diversified way.

American church buildings have many faces. Architecturally, they reflect the people's aspirations as well as their geographic location. Most common in America is the little white church with its steeple tapering to the sky and leading man's view upward in hope and faith.

Arguing the matter one day with Episcopalian Patrick Henry, whose only fear was that the Constitution did not sufficiently protect religion, Madison said:

Happily for the States, they enjoy the utmost freedom of religion. This freedom arises from that multiplicity of sects which pervades America, and which is the best and only security for religious liberty in any society. For where there is a variety of sects, there cannot be a majority of any one sect to oppress and persecute the rest.

So far from deploring or quaking at this diversity, the Founders saw it as a guarantee against any repetition of the sorry and scandalous State-Church relationships from which they had fled. But might not this very freedom give rise to unworthy groups? Jefferson had no fears about that; it would be taken care of in the democratic manner! He said: "If a sect arises whose tenets would subvert morals, good sense has fair play and reasons and laughs it out of doors, without suffering the State to be troubled with it."

American Protestantism, with its more than two hundred and fifty denominations, has its critics. From abroad, as well as from Americans who have yet to be imbued with the spirit of democracy and religious liberty, comes scornful reference to our "vast proliferation of sects." Actually, however, it is not Protestantism's diversity but its lack of *uniformity* that disturbs the critics.

It was uniformity in religion that the Founders feared and fought against, legislated against. Jefferson scorched "the impious presumption" of those who, "being themselves but fallible and uninspired men, have assumed dominion over the faith of others, setting up their own opinions and modes of thinking as the only true and infallible." And of his fellow-seekers after religious liberty he demanded: "Is uniformity of opinion desirable? No more than

Although some big city edifices, like New York's Trinity Church, are crammed between cliffs of tall edifices, their shadows dominate "the crowded ways of life."

Many Protestant houses of worship are patterned after colonial church models. The style of the meetinghouse, preserved in some contemporary churches, has influenced modern church structures.

of face and stature. Difference of opinion is advantageous to religion. The several sects perform the office of a *censor morum* over each other. Is uniformity attainable? Millions of innocent men, women and children, since the introduction of Christianity, have been burnt, tortured, fined, imprisoned; yet we have not advanced one inch toward uniformity. What has been the effect of coercion? To make one half of the world fools, and the other half hypocrites. To support roguery and error all over the earth."

Has Protestantism in America departed from its original thumbs-down on uniformity as a way to unity? Not by an iota. The thumb's firm downward direction was indicated when Bishop G. Bromley Oxnam (Methodist) said recently: "If I had to give up my liberty to gain unity, I would prefer to keep my liberty!" Or when Charles P. Taft, first layman president of the Federal Council of the Churches of Christ in America, declared: "Compelling uniformity is a confession not of strength but of weakness. The unity which would be uniformity is no aim which modern men who have had a taste of real democracy will ever accept." In short, Americans will never goose-step to heaven any more readily than they will goose-step any-

Plain folk in the "back country" villages usually are members of small but deeply devoted congregations, meeting in simple houses of worship. These are centers of social and civic life.

where else. The fifty million spiritual sons of Roger Williams are still echoing his trumpet-blast: "God requireth not an uniformity of religion!"

Unity within diversity is something else again. It is the Protestant's high goal, ever held before him. And recently he has been making long strides toward it. The critic who whines: "Why don't you Protestants get together?" needs to come alive and look around.

He needs to look first at Protestantism's diversity. If he looks carefully enough and objectively enough, his jeers may turn to cheers. In no other country is there such a rich pattern of religious life. Protestantism's 250,000 local congregations are planted in the obscurest places and "where cross the crowded ways of life." They fit the yearnings of ultraconservative, ultraliberal, and all between.

Their churches, built of their gifts of hands and heart, range in architectural style from vaulting cathedral to village church to storefront to tent. In the big city, in the little town, or set like a gem in the countryside, their sanctuaries, whether steepled or plain, Gothic or Colonial or modern, are an expression of their love for God and their fellow-man, of their aspirations for themselves and their communities.

In no other country will one find so rich and varied a pattern of religious life, order of worship and preference for devotional expression. In this pattern there is something to fit the yearnings of everyone from the ultraconservative to liberal.

In Protestantism's wide diversity of denominations there is room for him who likes his religion simple and unadorned, and for him who prefers his stately with ritual. Yet in all and through all runs the constant thread of unity of spirit, aim and aspiration.

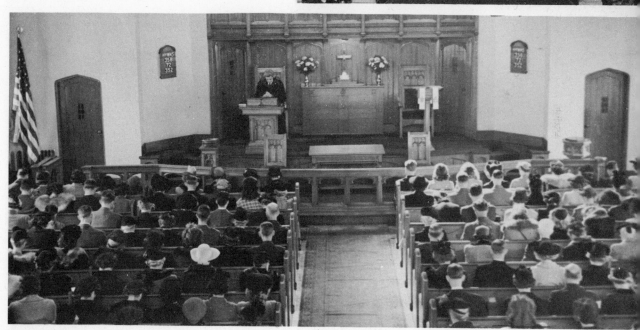

Protestant sanctuaries range in architectural style from the simplest to the most magnificent. This diversity one may see wherever he looks. In Protestantism, especially in the large centers, are many lovely structures where, with their artistic interiors, glistening marble and stained-glass windows, stately ritual and great music, the ministry of beauty is allied with the ministry of piety.

The growing practice of union services among Protestant communions on the local level is a vivid sign of increased "coming together." Such services—Lenten, Easter sunrise and others—have done much to promote Protestantism's essential unity amid diversity. The average Protestant wants not a "super church," now or ever, but he does want co-operative unity in fellowship and action. He is getting it today, more than ever before.

Within American Protestantism there is room for all, of whatever class or doctrinal persuasion.

There's room for the fellow who likes his religion heavy with creedal declarations and for him who eschews all written creed and wants his faith manifested in works. There's place for him whose main concern is the salvation of his soul, and for him who puts his emphasis on saving society; for him who likes his religion warm with emotion, and for him who prefers his stately with ritual. Conservative, liberal and middle-of-the-roader.

Yet American Protestantism is not nearly so diverse as it seems. In one-tenth of our two hundred and fifty denominations will be found 95 per cent of all America's Protestants. The top dozen denominations alone, each with a membership in excess of a million, account for 77 per cent of the whole. Four out of five American Protestants are allied to one of the six general divisions: Methodist, Baptist and Disciples, Lutheran, Presbyterian and Reformed, Congregational-Christian, and Protestant Episcopal.

Just as Protestantism's diversity is not nearly so conglomerate as it seems, so has its disunity been vastly exaggerated. He who would give the Protestant picture as that of so many embattled pups, huddling jealously over their respective bones of contention, and growling ominously at others over theirs, is using an old

No feature in a Reformation Day service is more prominent than the open Bible, carried in processional by representatives of all races and nationalities—signifying Protestantism's acceptance of, and dependence upon, the Holy Scriptures.

tintype, taken a hundred or more years ago. While there are still some Protestant groups which stand ready to do battle at the drop of a dogma, the vast majority of American Protestants have outgrown their suspicions and rivalry. Most have long ago discovered that, as Theodore Roosevelt (Dutch Reformed) once commented: "There are plenty of targets to hit without firing into each other!"

In the beginning it was inevitable that rivalries, intolerance, bigotry and fierce isolationism should exist between sects. These are the first signs of any body newly born to liberty—whether that body be religious, political, social or whatnot. The childhood of freedom exhibits strange and baffling phenomena. The childhood of American Protestantism was no different. Sects argued, fought, quarreled, made wild claims for themselves as having "the one true faith"—and, rejoicing in their liberty to do so, split all over the place.

American Protestantism today may be said to be in its late adolescence and early maturity. Whereas in its childhood it spoke, understood and acted like a child, it now has largely put away childish things. The dissensions and rivalries are now, on the whole, outgrown and discarded.* And certainly in Protestantism today there are seldom heard claims that the whole State and society should be subject to its sole influence and control, as do the Romanists and

---

* Unfortunately, and contrary to general opinion, disunity among religionists, now largely outgrown in Protestantism, is by no means peculiar to Protestants. One can find quite as much, perhaps even more, bitter rivalry between Roman Catholic orders and national groupings—viz., Jesuits and Dominicans, Benedictines and Redemptorists, Irish and German and Italian Catholics—as were ever manifest in Protestantism. That Catholic dissensions do not get to the public is due to the hierarchy's ability to enforce silence when they become too vituperative. Behind the scenes, however, there is more divisiveness than there ever was between Protestant sects, who fought, when they did fight, out in the open, with no holds barred and no shades drawn.

In great centers across America, Protestant communions frequently get together for the observance of impressive "festivals of faith," union services and special Reformation Day ceremonies. Often the cities' largest auditoriums overflow in these demonstrations of unity and strength. Such gatherings frequently lead to united action in many areas of human need.

as once did the Lutherans and Anglicans. The Spirit of the living God, along with the spirit of democracy, has refined that sophomoric arrogance out of Protestantism. To the vast majority of Protestants, denominational labels are that and little else. They identify a man with a tradition or a worship practice wherein he feels comfortable, or they are convenient groupings for administrative purposes. As of now, the division between conservatives and liberals is the only major wall separating Protestants from each other. And it is significant that this wall is not so much between sects as between interdenominational groupings.

As between denominations, the walls have come tumbling down. They are still tumbling. Not only has schism virtually ceased within denominations, and the multiplication of new sects has almost come to a standstill, but churches formerly separated have been rushing back to the remarriage altar. Everywhere in American Protestantism the signs of organic consolidation are out. In the past forty years, no fewer than fourteen major unions or reunions have been consummated, an average of one every three years.

Most impressive of the reuniters are the Methodists. The followers of John Wesley got a comparatively late start in America. The first Methodist preachers landed in 1769, a century

Laymen's retreats and joint brotherhood meetings bring together men of all Protestant faiths, who find communion together and foster fellowship across denominational lines.

and a half after the Pilgrims. Two years later, when the indefatigable Francis Asbury strode down the gangplank with far visions in his eyes, there were only six preachers in all the thirteen colonies; only six hundred members. But Methodism's men on horseback soon corrected that. The circuit riders flung themselves at the frontiers, and Methodists sprouted wherever the hoofs of their thundering herd beat out the Gospel advance. Whatever John Wesley, Anglican Tory to the last, lacked in appreciation of the American spirit of religious free enterprise, hard-riding Asbury and scholarly Thomas Coke and kindred spirits made up for it; on Christmas Eve, 1787, the American Methodist Church, independent of England, was formed. Today Methodist membership is close to nine millions. But in Methodism's rapidly growing house there was a skeleton in the closet. During the 1800's, this church had split three ways: into the Methodist Episcopal Church; the Methodist Episcopal Church, South; and the Methodist Protestant Church. Leaders of the three groups worked and prayed arduously over that skeleton. In 1939 they met in Kansas City's big convention hall, joyously reunited to form Protestantism's biggest family all under one roof, and, flinging their arms over each other's shoulders, made the rafters ring with "We are not divided, all one body we!"

The Methodists proved it could be done, with happiness and prosperity for all. They were by no means alone. The Congregationalist and Christian churches had recognized in each other a family likeness, and in 1931 promptly merged. They liked the arrangement, and when in 1949 it seemed that the Evangelical and Reformed (itself the product of a recent union) was ready for a proposal, the Congregational-Christians voted 757 to 172 in favor of the marriage—a union temporarily blocked only by court action on the part of dissenters. Like-

wise, in 1946 the United Brethren in Christ merged with the Evangelical United Brethren.

Many other groups, large and small, are talking union: Presbyterians of North and South, Northern (now American) Baptists and Disciples, Methodist and Protestant Episcopal. Southern Baptists, seven millions strong and historically given to keeping their own company and counsel, are seriously talking with their Northern brethren about an all-encompassing Baptist alliance. Even the Lutherans, traditionally isolationist from the rest of the Protestant community (and from each other), are considering the union of three of their biggest bodies: American Lutheran, Evangelical Lutheran and United Lutheran. And, as a further token of the cracking isolationism of Lutherans today, note that the United Lutherans have joined the Augustana and Danish branches as active members of the new National Council of Churches.

On the local level, significant evidence of the tumbling walls of church division is seen in the growth and vitality of community churches. These result from the amalgamation of two or more churches in "overchurched" localities. The movement is widespread all across the land. More than four hundred such worshiping bodies are joined in informal fellowship within the International Council of Community Churches; there are many hundreds of others which have no ties other than to their own communities. And beside the independents, there is a growing tendency on the part of denominations to co-operate in the establishment of community churches, especially in rural sections, basing the decision of any such church's denominational affiliation upon the majority representation in the community.

Parenthetically, it should be noted that Protestants have been, and are now, more active than any others in seeking interfaith accord.

Convincing evidence of Protestant maturity is the co-operative unity manifest when representatives of different denominations get together to discuss their common goals and means of realizing them, as in this meeting of one of the many departments of the Federal Council of the Churches of Christ.

With the principle of tolerance deep in their strain, they have gone out of their way, in a hundred different directions, to promote brotherliness between Protestant, Roman Catholic and Jew. They have done so in the abiding conviction that religionists, of whatever faith, can and should find areas for co-operation in affairs important to the community and nation. This, they hold, can be accomplished without the surrender of any article of any creed.

You cannot dodge the evidence. Separatist tendencies, so far as Protestants are concerned, are a fading phenomenon; organic union groups with common heritage and convictions are one of the encouraging signs of the day. Nevertheless, it must be pointed out that organic union of the *whole* of American Protestantism is not imminent, however passionately some Protestants may yearn for it. The American tradition is too strong. Americans fear bigness and monopoly; many will always prefer the close fellowship of the small group. Above all, they fear anything that even looks like uniformity. The voices of Roger Williams and Madison and Jefferson still ring in their ears. Yet their unwillingness to surrender denominational sover-

In Protestantism, schism has virtually ceased, union and reunion of denominations is on the rise. Biggest of all the reuniters are the Methodists, which in 1939 brought together three separate bodies. Bishops of the three groups joined hands in token of their historic "all one body we" achievement.

eignty has not stunted their growth toward the larger maturity. To them, any amalgamation of machinery is no good—but the "communion of saints" is!

The truly convincing proof of Protestant maturity, therefore, is not in its several organic unions. Rather, it is in its *co-operative unity,* "unity within diversity." That is something to watch, something to thrill the soul. It has been building up for a long time. Many forces have contributed to it.

Students have had a lot to do with it. Stalwart old John Mott stalked the world and fired the imaginations of youth by the millions. Such interdenominational bodies as the Student Volunteer Movement, the United Christian Youth Movement, the Student Christian Association, the YMCA and YWCA taught students of various denominations how to join their separate torches into a conflagration of flaming Christianity that made greater sense as well as brighter light. Christian Endeavor was established in 1881, bringing great numbers of youth together. Missions, home and foreign, contributed immensely; facing alien cultures and heathenism, Protestants in these fields saw early how silly it was to remain apart. Local churches and ministerial associations, getting together for union Thanksgiving or Lenten services, or uniting to attack a political problem or social evil in the community, delightedly discovered ties of Christian love and common purpose they had never suspected before. Local councils of churches sprang up all over the land; there are now seven hundred of them. County and state and regional councils followed—and, naturally, national councils.

Early in the 1800's, local churches of different denominations began to form local Sunday-school unions; in 1824 the American Sunday School Union was formed. In 1872 the International Sunday School Association came into being to co-ordinate programs and church-school lesson materials for many denominations. The Foreign Missions Conference of North America was born the following year, the Home Missions Council fifteen years later. The Federal Council of the Churches of Christ in America was formed in 1908, with constituent denominations representing a thumping majority of all American Protestantism banded together "for the prosecution of work that can be better done in union than in separation." Other agencies, such as the Protestant Council on Higher Education, the United Stewardship Council and the United Council of Church Women, rapidly followed.

None of these was set up overtly to achieve organic union between sovereign denominations. Nor did they make the fatal error of conditioning their co-operative endeavors on creedal agreement, much less uniformity. Moreover, they were in no sense controlling bodies. They have no prerogatives relating to the internal affairs of their constituent denominations. To the strong denominationalist, those "limitations" were protection; to the lover of organic unity, they were handicaps. But to the average American Protestant, they added up to practical, hardheaded common-sense, fully in accord with the American tradition of free but federated co-operation practiced so successfully by the forty-eight states.

Somewhat slower to arrive at the maturity represented by co-operative action between denominations have been the miscellaneous smaller sects in Protestantism's variegated panorama. Mostly made up of churches with fewer than 50,000 members each, these represent less than 10 per cent of American Protestantism's total strength. They comprise, for the most part, the so-called "splinter groups" which separated from the larger churches for doctrinal reasons. They may lack numerical strength, but they are not at all shy on piety and a fervent loyalty to their interpretation of God's will for them. Some are declining; others are growing fast. While they have their differences, and are not slow to defend spiritually what they believe, their "peculiarities" and "contentions" have been vastly exaggerated. And their contribution to the vital religious life of America has often been far out of proportion to their numbers. Only the religious snob would deny them a place, and a suitably prominent one, in the total Protestant picture.

To these smaller sects must be added hundreds of thousands of conservatives within the larger denominations—and these are far more numerous than any statistics can properly suggest. Traditionally, they have been far more interested in the salvation of the individual soul than in the shaping of society's face. To them belongs much credit for keeping the evangelistic emphasis alive in Protestantism, for preserving the warmth and emotion of vital personal religion. From their ranks largely have arisen such significant movements as "Youth For Christ" and such phenomenally successful evangelists as Billy Graham.

Any unanimity of faith and works between the fundamentalist groups has, until recently, been limited to mutual admiration based on a common acceptance of the basic tenets of the Gospel and on techniques for spreading it. Lately, however, the conservatives and fundamentalists—in both small and large sects—have been making strides toward united action. Their "diversities" may be even wider than those of Protestants in the majority group, but they have been finding unity nevertheless. The National Association of Evangelicals, formed in 1943, claims the allegiance of some thirty-three "denominational associates," with a membership above a million; its actual constituency is much larger.

But whether conservative or liberal—the average Protestant in America—and there are many millions of him—wants no "super church," now or ever. He does want co-operative unity, in fellowship and action. He's getting it!

If he is a member of the majority wing, he stands to get more of it now. In November, 1950, after nine years of careful planning, twenty-nine Protestant and Eastern Orthodox communions put the capstone on their steadily arising arch of Christian co-operation by the creation of the National Council of the Churches of Christ in the U.S.A. This was the long-awaited merger of the eight major interdenominational agencies which for decades have been showing Protestants on all levels how co-operation can be effected on the topmost level. The eight bodies in the coalition are: the Federal Council, the Foreign Missions Conference, the Home Missions Council, the International Council of Religious Education, the Missionary Education Movement, the Protestant Council on Higher Education, the United Council of Church Women and the United Stewardship Council. Also merged with them are a string of such other specialized agencies as Church World Service and the Protestant Radio Commission.

No union of denominations, the National Council is distinctly a merger of their common interests. The Council is new, hence one cannot fully evaluate its potentialities. But if it doesn't accelerate the growth of "unity within diversity," if it doesn't cut down vastly on supervisory overhead and duplication, if it doesn't make for increased influence of American Protestantism through its "united front," if it doesn't draw all denominations closer together, provide a stronger voice for laymen in church affairs, become a clearing house for exchange of ideas and views aimed at development of a sound Protestant strategy, and supply a practical and convincing demonstration of the churches' desire for integrated action in the face of current world conditions, then it will miss the work set for it—and we will miss our guess.

On Sunday, December 3, 1950, the first Sunday in the life of the new Council, some 31,000,000 Protestants went to their knees to rededicate themselves to the task of "exalting the Christ who recognized no barriers of sectarian differences," and to pray for Pentecostal power to attend this newest and biggest "coming together" in American Protestantism's history.

One had better not discount such united yearning and prayer! Protestants have had a way of making their dreams come true. And God has had a way of answering prayer—especially when prayed in the spirit and for the sake of His Son who lived and died and rose again "that they might be one"! If "two or three gathered together" can bring the Universal Christ in, what might 31,000,000 accomplish?

The Protestant conscience on social evil and his impulse to constantly improve the good and banish the bad in society stems from the Master's declaration, "I am come that they might have life . . . more abundantly." A shining promise to the oppressed, that declaration was also a sharp threat to their oppressors. Spurred by its tremendous implications, Protestantism, through an infinitely varied program of relief, rehabilitation and reform, has brought back to the world the prophetic voice and the compassionate hand.

VII

PROTESTANT DESIGN AND SOCIAL DISORDER

The Protestant, when labels are being pasted, generally gets tagged as a "religious activist." The term is fancy but accurate. As contrasted with the "quietist," who subscribes to the idea that the world is evil and man can do nothing about it, the activist is a person alert, vigilant, exceedingly busy at the job of improving his world.

Next to his passion for personal religious freedom, and its propagation through evangelism and missions, the trait which most accurately sets a Protestant apart from others is his quick readiness to be about his Master's business in social welfare and reform. He is a born combination of Good Samaritan and Crusader. When he sees human distress in any form, he is constitutionally unable to avert his eyes. When he comes upon man's inhumanity to man, he cannot refrain from rolling up his sleeves and getting into the fight to end it. When he sniffs moral or political corruption, he cannot keep his feet from following his nose to the source, or restrain his hands from reaching out to shut off the stench. And he does so without waiting for anybody to draft him, or until some official board or commission or hierarchy identifies the enemy for him, plans the campaign and sounds the bugle.

Activist! That trait springs directly from the Protestant's sense of compassion, is inextricably tangled with his feeling for "brotherhood" and his responsibility for activating it. He comes by that feeling naturally, by divine appointment. It all goes back to the beginning, and to God's first questions to man—sharp questions, penetrating questions that fastened forever on mankind its primary responsibilities. "Where art *thou?*" was demanded of Adam, attempting to dodge responsibility for his individual sin. "Where is . . . *thy brother?*" was demanded of Cain, trying to edge out of his social accountability.

God has been putting those questions ever since, to every man, and in that order. The Protestant holds that a Christian is answerable first for his own personal spiritual status; next, and just as important, he is answerable for the souls of mankind. And when we try to shrug off that responsibility with a languid: "Am I my brother's keeper?" we get the reply fast and straight: "Thy brother's blood crieth unto me from the ground!"

As an activist, the Protestant is in the direct line of prophetic and apostolic succession. He is related to Moses, who denounced Pharaoh's oppression and rounded up the oppressed for

TOP
The Christian responsibility of the family, as the basic unit of our society, is constantly held before parents by pastors ministering to their flock.

LEFT
Into every field of life the Protestant minister carries his Gospel of the relationship of religious faith to the social order. In farm districts no man is more important than the rural pastor who brings to farmers and their families not only a sense of Christian fellowship but of their partnership with God in working the soil.

TOP
Instilling into the mind and heart of the laboring man his high duty to God and country, as a vital cog in the great machine that is Christian America, is the task of the industrial chaplain whose particular ministry is a rapidly expanding one in this modern age.

RIGHT
Many are the thousands of Protestant hospitals, institutions for the aged and infirm, orphans and indigent in America which minister to the sick and needy. In each, doctors and chaplains join their labors to bring both physical and spiritual recovery.

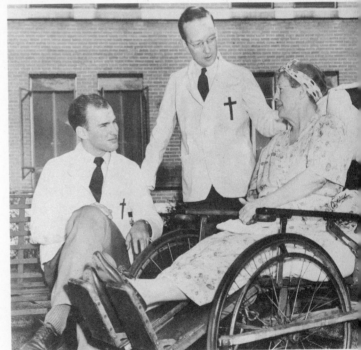

history's first labor walkout, then received direct from God a set of thunderous Commandments as pointedly social as they are personal. He is blood brother of all the old Hebrew prophets—of barefooted and flaming-eyed Amos, who swept down upon Jerusalem and hurled his rebukes at the easy evils of the day; of such scourgers of social and political sin as Elijah and Nehemiah and Jeremiah and Hosea and Micah; of the desert-hewn John, called the Baptist, whose rousing summons to repentance was in no wise restricted to individuals but was so pointedly aimed at high-placed sinners against the social order that they had to chop off his head to silence his tongue.

Stemming straight from the prophets came the Protestant's conscience on social evil. But direct from Jesus himself comes the cue for social action that is both ameliorative and rehabilitative. The cry of Jesus: "I am come that they might have life . . . more abundantly," was both promise and threat. Scathing was the Christ when facing those who preyed on the poor, the weak, the children. But while aiming His sharpest barbs at the oppressors, He turned

TOP
"In prison, and ye visited me" is the testimony of many in penal and correctional institutions where Protestant ministers and lay workers labor year in and year out to bring regeneration to society's rejects.

LEFT
"Into the highways and hedges" of big city life go compassionate Protestants daily, seeking to find and lead back to a respectable life those who somehow, often through no fault of their own, have become a drag and a menace instead of a "lifter" in modern society.

His tenderest compassion to their victims—healing the sick, frequenting the haunts of publicans and poverty-ridden, working his miracles for diseased and demoniac.

The Christ spirit infused those first disciples. The first appointees to churchly duty were deacons charged with looking after the sick and the needy, the widow and the orphan. Meanwhile, the apostles ranged the cities of the then known world, preaching a brand of brotherhood that aimed to set men right with God and society right with man.

Something bigger than military might had struck a weary world. It was Love and Brotherhood—and Justice. The tyrants could tolerate Love and Brotherhood; they were afraid of Justice. The great mailed fists that squeezed the world began to quail. This Christianity—it was ludicrous, laughable. But it was working. And though the tyrants stained the sands of their amphitheaters with Christian blood, though they beheaded, stabbed, flayed, hacked and burned and crucified, this new spirit spread and spread. The stones that dropped the martyrs became the foundation for institutions of

TOP
Rescue missions for the permanent rehabilitation of men who through their own weaknesses have gravitated to the hopeless alleys of the nation's "skid rows" is a prominent feature of Protestantism's multifarious program for transforming society's liabilities into assets.

RIGHT
Services and conveniences for seafaring men, such as New York City's famous Seamen's Church Institute, are provided in many American and foreign ports by Protestant institutions with an evangelical urge to help sailors keep their spiritual sea legs while enjoying "land liberty."

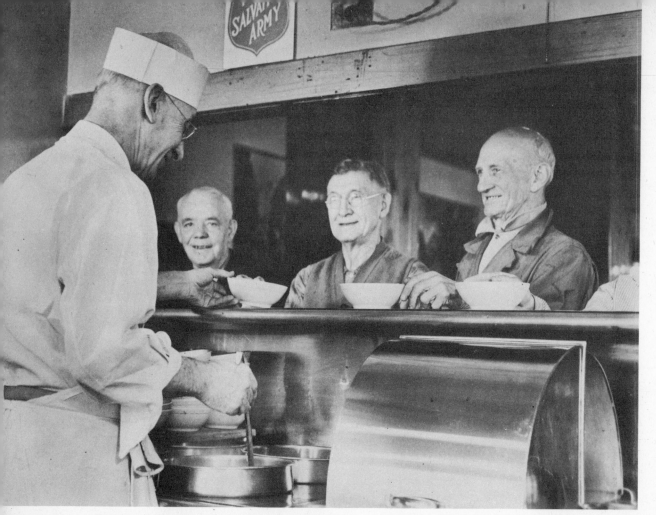

Canteens, industrial homes and institutions for the unemployed are maintained by the thousands in large and small towns all across America by the Salvation Army and other Protestant agencies. Here a man temporarily down discovers that he is by no means necessarily "out."

mercy. Martyrs' blood became the seed of a new order wherein all men were brothers and no man dared deny to another his rights.

Scholars may stumble over it. Psychologists may probe it. Historians may haggle over it. Ordinary mortals may sneer at it, laugh at it. But it was this new spirit, enunciated by the prophets and activated by Jesus, which has made the world over, again and again, and which will go on making it over. As long as Christians saw their world as the Master saw

it, their responsibility to that world as He stressed it, the Church Universal made strides in civilization such as had never been seen. Both Christianity and civilization went into a long eclipse when they lost it.

Protestantism brought back to the world the prophetic voice and the compassionate hand. In the van were the Waldenses, followers of Peter Waldo, first of all Protestants; then Martin Luther and John Calvin and John Knox. They struck blows for social and economic reform

"Unto one of the least of these" is the motto and the everyday practice of thousands of Protestant orphanages, day nurseries and child-care institutions who early introduce underprivileged little ones to Christian charity and a right start toward good citizenship.

that sent the tyrants scurrying and the oppressors stumbling. Up went orphanages, hospitals, havens for the indigent and the aged. They answered the aching agonies of the oppressed with Christian love and succor. It became a habit. By the time the first colonists arrived in the New World, they had been conditioned to accept the Lord's requirement, voiced by Micah: "Do justly, love mercy, walk humbly with thy God." It took them a while to activate that high directive fully, but it burned into their consciences until they did. Doing justly, they established a political society whose inner genius would stand forever opposed to injustice of any kind. Loving mercy, they created a philanthropic society that would become first among all nations for its open heart and liberal hand.

The scope of American Protestantism's quality of mercy strains the ability of any man to fully assess. Just try to count the hundreds of thousands of hospitals, institutions for the

(Continued on page 119)

PROTESTANT DESIGN AND SOCIAL DISORDER *115*

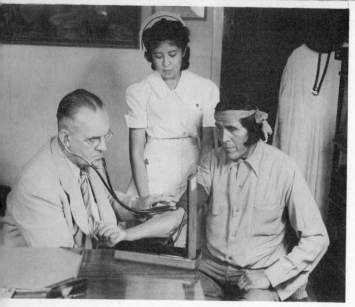

The problems of migratory workers have evoked a broad and socially significant Protestant program, conducted by denominational and interdenominational societies on a scale whose vastness is little realized by the average American. Such people, deprived of the rights and privileges belonging to a settled community, readily respond to the spiritual, medical and recreational services freely offered.

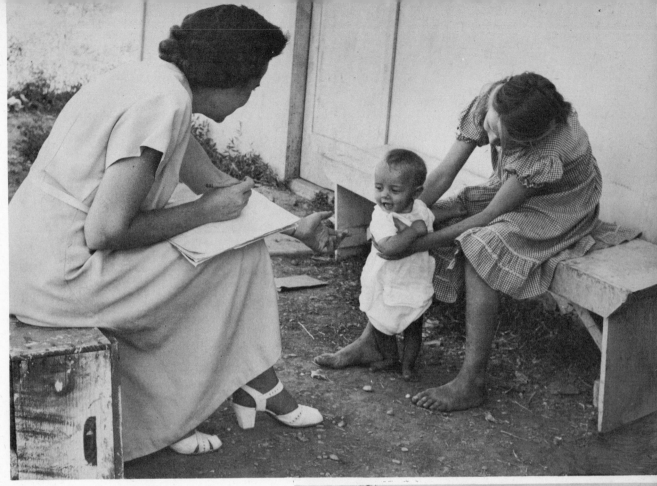

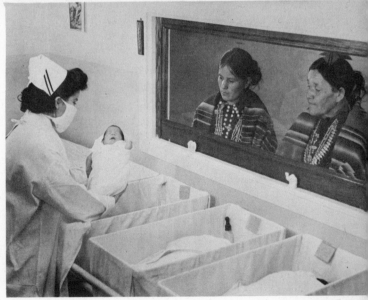

From the beginning of American history, when Roger Williams and William Penn fought for fair treatment of the Indians, the plight of the "first Americans" has stirred the compassion of Protestants who believe that missions, like charity, should begin at home. Under Protestant auspices, churches and schools and hospitals by the hundreds have been established for the red man on and near the reservations.

TOP LEFT

During and following World War II, American Protestant churches were deep in the effort to supply the orphaned and war-stricken of Europe and Asia with the necessities of life. In Christ's name, they sent uncounted shiploads of food, clothing and money to help the innocent victims of war to start anew.

TOP RIGHT

Into America since World War II have poured many thousands of displaced persons from the war-wrecked areas of Europe. Church World Service, interdenominational relief and rehabilitation agency for Protestant churches, meets these DPs whom they call "Delayed Pilgrims" at the wharf and follows through until their happy and gainful resettlement in America.

BOTTOM LEFT

Another service is that performed by the Mennonites, who donate and prepare their own food, manufacture their own cans and ship carloads of needed foodstuffs to Europe's hungry peoples.

BOTTOM RIGHT

In addition to the many-phased service conducted by Church World Service on behalf of Protestant denominations, many churches have their own specialized programs demonstrating the practical compassion of Christians. One sample is the "hatching eggs" project carried on by Church of the Brethren congregations. In this, hatching eggs are donated by Brethren farmers and shipped by fast plane to help restock stricken farms in Europe.

aged and infirm, the orphans and the indigent, rescue missions and relief stations that minister to the sick and needy in this land. A great percentage of them were begun, if not now maintained, under Protestant auspices and inspired by Protestant compassion. Long before the government became concerned with physical health, relief and rehabilitation, the Protestant churches had set up their institutions, trained their doctors and workers, and were busy and efficient at the job of succoring mankind on innumerable Jericho roads.

Today Protestants are busier than ever on those roads; they will always be busy there. Walk into the background of almost any project to alleviate human woe, religious or secular, and you cannot avoid bumping into Protestants all over the place. It will always be Christianity's task to minister, as did its Founder, to the needy, the sick, the mentally upset, the orphaned, the outcast, the victims of mankind's own weaknesses, the by-products of society's own failures.

In modern times, as in the days of the prophets, Protestantism is vigorously laying its sharp ax at the roots of social distress and disorder. While still busy gathering up society's derelicts and applying the rehabilitative grace of God to their restoration, it is demanding that attention be given to the things that wrecked them in the first place. While still carrying baskets of food and hampers of clothes to the hungry and naked, it is addressing pertinent questions as to why those baskets and hampers are necessary. While walking the alleys of slums and the wards of institutions of all kinds, it is searching for causes and calling for solutions.

The present Protestant mood, strong and growing stronger by the hour, is that rescuing brands from the burning is a necessity, but putting out the fire makes more sense. If bandaging

As the result of cultivation by CROP, the interdenominational Christian Rural Overseas Program, nearly three thousand carloads of friendship cargo —including grains, dairy products, livestock, soybeans, raw cotton and wool—are sent out each year as the gift of Christian farmers in America to orphanages, hospitals, institutions for the aged and refugee agencies in Europe and Asia.

up the wounds of men torn by beasts of prey is good religion, doing something about the beasts is better.

To the Protestant, the vision of right always on the scaffold, wrong always on the throne, with an impotent God helplessly watching over his own, may make poetry, but it hardly squares with the prophets or with Jesus and their activism on behalf of a better world and a more abundant life.

As never before, Protestantism is tackling the unclean spirits which, left unchallenged, make the world a breeding ground for malice and hatred and greed and prejudice and exploitation. The evil spirits don't relish that. Like those exorcised by Jesus, they come forth screaming. You hear their cries: "Let Christians mind their business of saving souls!" Christians reply: "That's precisely what we *are* doing—minding souls, the soul of man and the soul of society."

Whatever the social evil, there have always been Protestants to stand up to it and call it by name, echoing the Nazarene's: "I command

To give children too a part in building friendship ties across oceans, and thus erecting firm foundations for world brotherhood and a firm social order, Church World Service has its "World Friendship Among Children" movement. Gifts sent abroad represent the sharing of the children's own toys, games and candies with the needy ones in lands raked by war's destruction and poverty.

thee, come out!"—often with spectacular results.

That cry resounded from the pulpits and platforms of Jonathan Edwards, Samuel Hopkins, Phillips Brooks, Theodore Parker, T. DeWitt Talmadge, Henry Ward Beecher, C. H. Parkhurst, John B. Gough, Frances Willard, Washington Gladden—and is heard in tens of thousands of rostrums today. It shouted from the theology of Nathaniel Taylor, Charles G. Finney, Timothy Dwight, Josiah Strong, Francis G. Peabody, Shailer Matthews, Walter Rauschenbusch—and is echoed in the books and classrooms of virtually every present-day theologian. It permeated the writings of such of America's Protestant literary lights as James Russell Lowell, Henry George, William Lloyd Garrison, John Greenleaf Whittier, Harriet Beecher Stowe, and makes dramatic and socially significant the works of America's best-selling poets and novelists of this day.

The effort to make Christianity effective in the social, economic and political life of the nation has been especially noteworthy in the

The need for resettling in American Christian homes of European orphans from foreign lands is met easily when account is taken of Protestant compassion—as in the case of these four being "claimed" at the pier by their new father who, through the services of his church, learned of their availability. Many thousands of war orphans have thus found new and permanent parents, who will bring them up in the Christian faith.

In no area of social reform has Protestantism been more active than in the field of temperance. Such interdenominational organizations as the Woman's Christian Temperance Union join with denominational and civic-reform groups to battle this and other social evils on every front. They draft their entire personnel and draw their biggest support from churches committed to banishing evils inevitably following liquor's misuse.

In the Protestant view, while it is good to bandage up the wounds of men and women torn by anti-social conditions, it is better to do something about the conditions. In every community Protestants are found battling political corruption, juvenile and **adult delinquency, race and religious prejudice, gambling and vice. Many groups work ceaselessly at the legislative level, influencing politicians to be statesmen and forcing elected officials to fulfill their vows.**

past half-century. In 1908, at a time of yeasty social ferment, the Methodists brought out their "Social Creed." Later that year, the Federal Council of the Churches of Christ in America was formed, representing thirty-three denominations; as one of its first actions it adopted, in expanded and italicized form, the Methodist statement, calling it the "Social Creed of the Churches." This creed pulled no punches in declaring for equal rights and justices for all men; the abolition of child labor; the abatement of poverty and the liquor traffic;

a fair break for workers, and a new application of Christian principles to the acquisition and use of property. Today most of the Protestant denominations, large and small, embody in their official statements of purpose ringing phrases right out of the prophets' mouths. Even those who reject the "social gospel" as a term practice it as a principle.

The Protestant conscience is a redoubtable fighter wherever you find it. In every community you will find it battling political corruptions, juvenile and adult delinquency, race and religious prejudice, liquor and gambling and vices of all sorts, fostering Christian tolerance and understanding, drawing together divergent groups, standing four-square for democracy. In rural life it is equally manifest, laboring for farm and home betterment, promoting Christian co-operatives. In medicine and science Protestant doctors and technicians, free and responsible, have come up with many of the major discoveries affecting the health and welfare of all the world. In industry its industrial chaplains and its church-labor representatives are constantly bringing better rapport between management and workers, between all men and their God.

And mark this: all that Protestants have done and are doing in all fields—relief, reform or rehabilitation—is done with an eye single to the betterment of society as a whole. They have never approached any social task with a Protestant ax to grind, a Protestant profit to accrue, a Protestant interest to serve.

Against all those tensions that tear at the heart of society, Protestantism has lifted its standard. It is the standard of true *brotherhood,* fastened firmly to the principle of a good life for all—not only for Protestants but for all men everywhere. It sees the world crisis clear, without the astigmatism that comes from selfish seeking for itself alone. It knows that Communism's success in today's world is a monument to the failure of Christians to accept their responsibility. It knows that Karl Marx stole from the Hebrew-Christian tradition its emphasis on the social aspirations of mankind, twisted that tradition into a brutal and heretical religion of its own. It knows that the battle with Marxism, or any other godless "ism," will be won only by the implementation everywhere of Judeo-Christian concepts.

It knows too that the battle of Christianity with the world's unclean spirits is a battle never-ending. For all the advances Protestantism has made, for all the unclean spirits cast out, there are new advances to be made, new devils to exorcize. Today, on the home front, it is the evil spirits that breed personal vices, economic inequity, social and political corruption, unbrotherly conduct toward men of other races and religions. On the world front, it is Communism, imperialism, war and the threats thereof. Tomorrow—something else. The battlefield changes, the enemy adopts new guises. But essentially he is the same devil—the devil of greed, selfishness, exploitation.

Full victory will not come overnight, not in a month or a year, perhaps not in a hundred years. But Protestants know that ultimate victory is theirs. They will lay down their arms only "when the kingdoms of this world shall become the Kingdom of our Lord and His Christ." Not before!

America is properly proud of its vast system of public education, broadest and most advanced in the modern world, one of American democracy's most signal achievements. Too often forgotten, however, is the fact that our educational system is the child of American Protestantism. Today Protestants are battling to preserve it against the onslaughts of those who would scuttle its heritage.

VIII

"WITH ALL THY MIND"

In any listing of the prime bulwarks of American democracy, you will find our free public schools close to the top. When the Protestant founders of this nation stepped onto these shores, their first act was to establish a home. Next, they erected a place of worship. Then they started a school. Out of the third in that trinity of interests has come not alone the finest and broadest and freest system of education to be found anywhere on earth, but out of it has come, in large part, the "American Way" as we know it.

That the American educational system is the child of American Protestantism is a byword with historians. Yet it is a fact too foggy in the minds of many citizens. They need to be reminded.

The Puritans and the Pilgrims came to the New World with a mind-set on the subject of education. In the lands they had left, education was the privilege of the few; they would make it the privilege—nay, the duty—of all. They distrusted illiteracy with the distrust of men and women who have seen what clerical-imposed ignorance could do in fettering a people. They knew that if men were to be free, self-governing, they must be enlightened.

In their hearts were Divine injunctions. "Know the truth," Jesus had said. "The truth shall make you free!" That's the way freedom would come, the only way it could come. "Thou shalt love the Lord thy God with all thy . . . *mind!*" The mind shackled and in fear can love nothing, much less God, and can create nothing, much less a nation.

So those early Americans flung up their rude schoolhouses on the New England shores, dotted them all along the advancing frontier. When vicious Indian raids burned the schools down, they built them again, invited the Indians to come inside and learn better, dispatched teaching missionaries out to instruct as well as evangelize the savages. In charge of these first schools they put the only educated ones among them—the preachers; the preachers, in turn, raised up dedicated men and women whose first thought was to found a generation of people fit to be free.

Their first textbook was the Bible, their first job to teach children to read. That was something new to pedagogy, new and vastly significant. In European schools, all instruction was oral; the pupil had to take his knowledge from the mouth of the teacher, was limited in his learning by what that mouth chose to speak. America's new *reading* schools were a long leap away from controlled thought, a far step toward unfettered thinking.

Another long step, vastly important to our evolving public-school system, was this: the

American public schools impress upon young minds the American principle of fair play, of due regard for other faiths and races, the moral and cultural codes of good behavior that lead to good citizenship.

The modern classrooms in America's free schools teach pupils to think for themselves, to express their own developing minds and skills. In our public elementary and secondary schools, twenty-six million pupils are learning the basic tenet of democracy: how to work with and respect others of all races and creeds. Today's schools, due to sinister attacks by secularists and some religionists, are weak in imparting religious knowledge while impressively strong in academics.

schools were governed by the community, not the church. Even though fervent religionists were at first in charge, they taught as representatives of the secular, not the religious, order. Separation of Church and State in educational matters? It was there from the beginning. Also enunciated, right in the beginning of America's unique public-school system, was the principle that *public funds were to be expended only on schools under public authority,* and that no religious sect should share in any way in such funds. Mark that principle; we shall see it attacked later.

But there was no separation of *religion* from education. The colonists would not brook that.

The first school law of Massachusetts, leader among the states in getting public education under way, ordered the selectmen to see that "all children are taught the principles of religion." And in 1787 the ordinance for the Northwest Territory echoed the New England policy by declaring: "Religion, morality, and knowledge, being necessary to good government and the happiness of mankind, schools and the means of education shall forever be encouraged." Protestants have always ditched their differences to maintain America's great institutions. They did so—gloriously—to found our public schools. In a time of more sectarian dissension than anywhere evident today, these

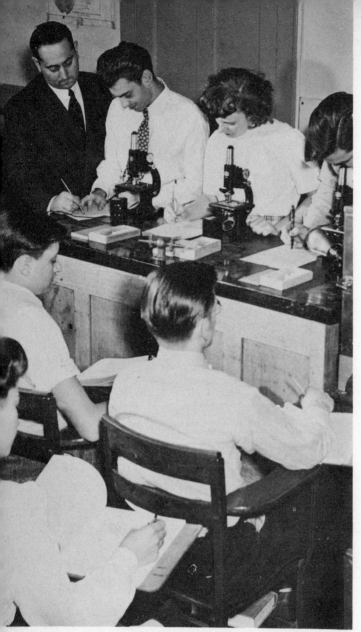

"Know the truth," Jesus said. "The truth shall make you free!" Strong in the scientific approach, our schools teach their pupils not only to think for themselves but to be forever probing, researching, evaluating evidences. This spirit of free inquiry, nurtured by Protestantism, has developed American science to unparalleled heights, is forever developing American youth that are informed and therefore free, intelligently free, responsibly free.

early Americans proved that religion could be taught without dogmatic bias.

Not only was the Bible prominent, but when the first secular texts appeared they were filled with moral maxims hot off the biblical griddle. Look up those early "readers"; find there the copious quotations from the Ten Commandments, the Lord's Prayer, the Psalms. Illustrated with Bible pictures, they taught the ABC's with such sayings as: "In *A*dam's fall, we sinned all" . . . "Heaven to find, the *B*ible mind" . . . "*C*hrist crucified for sinners died."

One well-known speller, published in 1676, boasted in its introduction: "By this book a lad may be taught to read a chapter in the Bible perfectly in a quarter of a year's time." Noah Webster's spellers and the McGuffey readers were replete with moral and religious sentiments. And for more than a hundred years, as a child advanced through the grades he met those same sentiments on every hand, in the writings of America's great poets and novelists, historians and jurists, artists and orators.

Not only did these religion-activated, freedom-motivated Protestants found our elementary schools, available to all, free to all. They founded also our first and foremost institutions of higher learning. Sixteen years after the Pilgrims landed, Harvard College came into being; its motto: "For Christ and the Church." Yale was founded in 1701 by a group of Congregational preachers for the purpose of preparing men for church and civil service; Princeton was established as an expression of yearning for education by the Presbyterian "revivalist party." Columbia, which came into being in 1754 as King's College, had a congregational minister as its first prexy, and a charter based on the convictions "in which, true Christians of each denomination are generally agreed." The University of Pennsylvania stemmed di-

Modern public education is rapidly catching up with biblical teaching that the care and development of the body, as the temple of the spirit, is quite as important as the training of the mind.

Through body-building courses and classes in health education, American youth learns the necessity of physical fitness as the prerequisite to a meaningful and useful life as parent and citizen.

TOP LEFT

First teachers of our public schools were Protestants committed to raising up a generation of people fit to be free. Their first textbook was the Bible, their first task to teach children to read for themselves, a far step toward unfettered thinking. These early Protestants made their schools available to all, free to all, which is the pattern today.

ABOVE

The Puritans and Pilgrims distrusted illiteracy, knew that if men were to be free they must be enlightened. So they flung up their rude schoolhouses all along the advancing frontier, hard by their log churches and worship centers.

LEFT

A hundred or more years ago the public school was strong in moral and religious precepts, though by today's standards they were weak in diversified curricula and equipment.

rectly from George Whitefield's electrifying preaching in Philadelphia during the Great Awakening; on the campus today, Founder Ben Franklin's statue is hard by that of Whitefield, "The Great Awakener."

These are but a few. For many decades there was virtually no higher education in America save that provided by the Protestant churches. Protestantism began its schools with a firm and fierce faith in the things it stood for. It cradled them, however, in tolerance and charity for all. Into the charters of their colleges went words like those of Union's, first college to be chartered west of the Hudson River: "This institution shall never exclude any person of any religious denomination from equal liberty and the advantage of education."

Born with a passion for truth, free and unfettered, American Protestantism has never lost it. Today it has some 475 church-supported colleges and universities. Many of them are among the foremost schools of the land. And a whopping percentage of those now under state or purely secular control got their start as church institutions.

Deeply rooted in the Protestant tradition, these schools did much to keep the new nation's morality from degenerating into mere sentiment, its commerce into greed, its politics into anarchy. No less an historian than Henry Steele Commager states flatly: "Our schools have kept us free." He goes on to say: "In our generation today, when the critical pedant of the Old World disparages American academic traditions, we are prone—and with much reason—to answer tartly: *it has never been the Americans who succumbed to the evil and meretricious appeals of Fascism, Nazism or Communism!*" Protestantism, militant believer in "the glory of the lighted mind," gave the United States that bulwark.

There seems to be more than coincidence in the fact that wherever Protestantism has been strong, literacy has flourished; and where it is weak, illiteracy abounds. One has but to compare the literacy ratings of England and Italy, the Scandinavian countries and Spain, Finland and Portugal, North America and Latin America, to get the point.

Proud is America today of her vast system of public education, broadest and most advanced in the modern world. Proud too are Protestants that, under the aegis of their great free tradition, that system arose to unparalleled heights of academic competence. Proud are all Americans of their public elementary and secondary schools giving instruction to 26,000,000 students annually. Proud are we all (while wishing it were more) of our part in providing five billion dollars annually of public funds to support these schools. And especially proud (while a bit conscience-stricken that we require it of them) are we of the selfless dedication of 990,000 classroom teachers, principals and supervisors, who, despite salaries that are on a par with those of unskilled laborers, nevertheless devote their high talents uncomplainingly to the making of more and better Americans. The public-school system, handicapped and harried though it be, is one of American democracy's most signal achievements.

Completely sold upon its merits, Protestants for almost a century now have been exporting the American brand of education to home mission fields and to a hundred lands beyond the sea. The Protestant churches, more than any other central agency of mankind, have been spearheading the drive against ignorance, superstition and illiteracy the world around. Protestantism, in exporting education, has outclassed the field. It is sponsoring today nearly 57,000 schools in the far corners of the world, not including those in Europe and North America. Of these, 53,000 are elementary schools;

1,200 are high schools; 102, colleges; 14, medical schools; 129, theological seminaries; 260, normal schools. That's an expression of faith for you!

But while the American education system has reached a peak in efficiency, something has happened to its heart. Protestants are facing this curious anomaly: religion, which founded the public schools, made them free, has largely been elbowed out. And across the land parents and educators themselves are disturbed by the epithets being flung at the schools: "Godless! Secular! Pagan!"

What, precisely, has happened? And how?

The blame has been placed by some on the "increasing secularity" of American life; upon the "unreligious influence" of Horace Mann, foremost prophet of American education; upon the "growing godlessness" of science; upon the "pragmatism" of John Dewey, chief formulator of modern educational theory; upon the employment in the teaching profession of persons with only a marginal interest in religion.

We wouldn't dismiss these "explanations" with a wave of the hand. There is some truth to them, though not much. We would point out that the dereligioning of public schools began at a period when the devotional and evangelical spirit was high, about the middle of the nineteenth century. We would further point out that Mann and Dewey, and especially Mann, were not the irreligionists their detractors claim. And that, most assuredly, the teaching profession is, on the whole, as spiritually sound a profession as any in the land; many teachers are outstanding churchmen, Christian youth leaders on the side, Sunday-school workers and the like.

To state the cause as flatly as the historical record itself states it: *the schools began to lose their religion when the Protestant belief in free public schools was met head-on by the designs of the Roman Catholic clergy against them.* If that seems harsh to men of tolerance and good will, let them look at the record.

By the turn of the nineteenth century, religion and education, with the aid of Christian men in both fields, had wrought a workable rapport—satisfactory to the sincerest tenets of both and to the utmost claims of the "separation of Church and State" principle. Religion, though not sectarianism, had a place in the curriculum. The Bible was read in most schools daily; prayers were made and hymns sung at opening exercises. Some states made such religious observances obligatory.

Then, between 1820 and 1850, began the huge waves of immigration from Europe. The rising tide brought two to eight millions of immigrants during each decade—and the schools had the terrific job of Americanizing the newcomers. It wasn't easy, for the immigrants came largely from political and religious cultures foreign to freedom. And, unlike those who founded America, their hunt was not for religious and political freedom primarily. They came seeking economic opportunity.

American schoolmen could and did Americanize these children of the immigrants politically and socially. But the immigrants' faith was something else again. Particularly hard to handle were those from Catholic Ireland and Catholic parts of Germany. Their illiteracy was high, their antipathies to Protestants strong. These "fighting Irish," naturally enough in view of their background, viewed all Protestants in the light of their alleged "oppression" under Protestant English rule. Many were rough and tough, and they slammed their way into politics in the big cities where they tended to congregate, agitating not so much for America's traditional religious and political freedom as for Irish freedom.

Clashes with the predominantly Protestant

As long ago as the **middle of the nineteenth century**, public schools were enlarging their scope to include classes for adults who had missed schooling as children. Today's classes for adults include many subjects: marriage and parenthood, domestic science, manual training, college preparation, art appreciation. Especially for immigrants not hitherto privileged to enjoy free education, there are, in addition to elementary schooling, classes in American citizenship and all it means in liberty and justice and tolerance for all.

Protestant-born, Harvard College came into being sixteen years after the Pilgrims arrived. Its first motto: "For Christ and the Church!" The original endowment was 800 pounds.

population were inevitable—especially when the Roman Catholic priests and bishops began to make loud and large demands for public funds to build parochial schools. The hierarchy, then as now, made no bones about its unqualified opposition to public schools. Part of irrevocable church law is Canon 1374, which flatly states:

The frequenting of non-Catholic schools, whether neutral or mixed, those namely which are open to Catholics and non-Catholics alike, is forbidden to Catholic children . . . and can be at most tolerated, on the approval of the Ordinary [bishop] alone, under determined circumstances of time and place, and with special precautions.

With that canon before them, Roman Church apologists have understandably gone all out in the endeavor to sell the parochial school to Catholic parents. In a pamphlet bearing the imprimatur of Cardinal Hayes, and never repudiated by the hierarchy, Father Paul L. Blakely stated:

The first duty of every Catholic father to the public school is to *keep his children out of it*. . . . The only school, whether it be a kindergarten or a university, which is fit for a Catholic, is the school that is Catholic in its principles, its aims, its programs, its teachers, and in its submission to the direction and supervision of the Church. . . . *"Every Catholic child in a Catholic school,"* is the command of the Church. . . . Discussion is at an end. The obligations imposed by obedience are alone to be considered.

Back in the middle 1800's, the only measure open to the American hierarchy was to get

Princeton was founded in 1746 by the Presbyterian "revivalist party," whose members were convinced they would be better evangelists if better educated. Like Harvard, its heritage is Protestant.

enough parochial schools built to house the influx. Hence the demand for public funds—a demand which was rigidly denied, on the same principle that it had been denied to all other private schools. Catholic parents, meanwhile, were sending their children to the public schools. Roman Catholic leaders, notably Archbishop John Hughes, then began bitter attacks against the public-school system—attacks which continue to the present day. The Bible (King James Version) was denounced as "a sectarian book." Objections were made to "Protestant" hymns and prayers used in opening exercises. Even recitation of the Lord's Prayer was frowned upon, unless Catholics in public schools stopped at the phrase, "For Thine is the kingdom"; the explanation is that "in practice these words have taken on a Protestant connotation," and their use would constitute "an implicit approval of heresy."

American teachers, most of them Protestant, were nonplused. Many at first refused to be badgered into making their schools even more secular than they already were. But others, sincerely trying to live up to the "separation" ideal, began to drop Bible-reading and other traditional religious observances.

Roman Catholic leaders thereupon began to raise the cry that the schools were "godless," and to campaign the more fervently for public support of parochial schools, so that "the conscience of Catholics will not be violated." Also, Catholic parents were repeatedly warned that sending their children to the public schools was

(Continued on page 140)

Columbia, founded in 1754 "for free and independent research and study," is the largest university in the modern world, with 40,000 students and 3,000 faculty members. Its first president was a Congregational minister and its charter was based on convictions "in which true Christians are generally agreed." Its domed library, containing nearly two million volumes, and its St. Paul's Chapel crowded with students seeking religious inspiration are more than landmarks on the campus.

The University of Pennsylvania came into being in 1740 as a direct result of the Rev. George White-field's preaching in Philadelphia. His statue is hard by that of Benjamin Franklin on the campus.

tantamount to inviting their ruin of soul, "and to do so while there is a good and well-equipped Catholic school in the place" would put them beyond the pale where absolution could be obtained.

Public funds for parochial schools did not become available. Again and again through the years, the hierarchy's bid for tax funds for their schools has been denied, often as the result of court action or state legislation. But the hierarchy never quit trying; they haven't yet.

In 1842 they took the fight to the polls in New York, forming a separate political organization with their own candidates pledged to get money for parochial schools. The result was defeat for the candidates and a legislature pledged more firmly than before to the principle of "No public funds for sectarian schools; no sectarian doctrines in the public schools."

Yet the pressure never let up. In the 1870's, it was applied to national politics. President Grant, speaking in Des Moines in September,

1875, left nobody in the dark as to where he stood. "Let us encourage free public schools," he shouted, "and resolve that *not one dollar* appropriated for their support shall be appropriated to the support of any sectarian school!" And in the national election 1876, the Republican Party inserted this plank in its platform:

The public school system of the several States is the bulwark of the American Republic; and with a view to its security and permanence, we recommend an amendment to the Constitution of the United States forbidding the application of any public funds or property for the benefit of any school or institution under sectarian control.

No new thing is federal aid to education; it came up to the Congress in the 1870's and 1880's. And no new thing is the Roman Catholic Church's opposition to it, save with the proviso that it get a share. Federal aid, then as now, was therefore stymied. Nor is the current plea for "auxiliary services" anything new. The Congress in 1896 and 1897 reacted with this expression of national policy, which conforms to the policy of most states:

It is hereby declared to be the policy of the Government of the United States to make no appropriation of money or property for the purpose of founding, maintaining, or *aiding by payment for services, expenses or otherwise,* any church or religious denomination, or any institution or society which is under sectarian or ecclesiastical control.

In 1917 the Smith-Hughes Act further reinforced the American stand against granting public moneys for "auxiliary services" by declaring:

No portions of any moneys appropriated under this Act for the benefit of the States shall be applied, *directly or indirectly* . . . for the support of any religious or privately owned or conducted school or college.

As the result of such forthright and repeated denials, on local, state and national levels, the persistent Roman Catholic attempts to crack America's historical stand have not availed. Yet the old battle, tirelessly renewed in every generation since 1840, goes on.

Nor have the threats to parents entirely availed. Many Catholic parents have seen the democratic advantages of having their children mingle freely with those of the Protestant and Jewish faiths. Today, though there are some 2,600,000 enrolled in 10,000 Roman Catholic parochial schools in America, there are just as many who are attending public schools. An increasing number of Catholic laymen, though voiceless before their church's stand against public schools, have been completely sold on them. Not so voiceless was at least one priest, who in 1889 dared to make his feelings known. Father Edward McGlynn (1837-99), afterward deposed for his "liberalism," though later restored, put his feelings on the line:

If I could reach the mind and the heart of the whole of the American people, I would say: Cherish your public schools; listen not to their enemies, no matter whence they come. Show no favor to any rival system. If you will not exercise the right to forbid rival systems altogether, at least do not be guilty of the incredible folly of nursing and fostering, and actually, by appropriations and tax exemptions, encouraging rival systems. The rival systems, as a rule, are promoted by those who, educated in foreign lands, are but half republican or but half democratic. Never be guilty of the folly of dividing your school fund among the various churches and sects. You, in such a case, would be guilty of destroying one of the greatest and most potent instruments for building up and maintaining one great, free, common nationality.

The good priest, good American, doubtless spoke the mind of many non-Protestants as well as his own. But he apparently made no converts among the top brackets of his church. The twin pressures against public schools and

OPPOSITE PAGE
Yale University got its start in 1701 as a school for Congregational preachers, later developed from a small New England college into one of the great educational centers of America.

ABOVE
Colleges and universities for Negroes, vitally important in raising the level of the race, almost without exception were established by Protestants —as were most of the secondary schools.

for some kind of tax support for Roman Catholic parochial schools continue unabated. Currently, the big drive is on to get some portion of the proposed federal aid to education allotted to Catholic schools for such "auxiliary services" as bus transportation, school lunches, textbooks —or to defeat the measure for all schools.

Early in the 1940's, it became plain that public education, if it were to maintain and progress, had to have some federal aid. Plaguing the states were teacher shortages, costs of maintenance, need for more facilities. Various bills have been proposed, and all have been vigorously opposed by the hierarchy except

those which include a slice for Roman Catholic parochial schools.

Educators in general, and Protestants in particular, see in Roman Catholic attempts to break the Church-and-State principle a consistency that would be admirable in any other cause. Exactly the same problems were faced between 1836 and 1848 by Horace Mann. As deeply religious as he was deeply devoted to the American tradition, Mann fought without stint and with success, as secretary for the Massachusetts Board of Education, to keep the schools clear of sectarian influence. Not always did he have support from even his Protestant

Weekday religious education, based on the "re-leased time" plan, was developed during the past two decades by Protestant leaders worried by the increased secularity of public schools. Operating in some 3,000 communities, this plan is helping reduce the threat of religious illiteracy.

fellow-educators; some had wearied in the battle, some were just apathetic to the threat. He sighed: "Men have become tolerant of intolerance."

Americans generally, looking around at their schools denuded of religion to the point of absurdity, are repeating Mann's lament today. More, they are shaping up a new and stiffened expression of the nub of American tradition. Stated simply, it is this:

America, through long and painful experimentation, has achieved a public-school system uniquely magnificent. It is free, it is democratic, it is available to everyone regardless of religion or race. But if any body of people do not choose to take advantage of its facilities, *preferring to set up their own system of schools, and if parents voluntarily choose to send their children to such schools, they have that right. But if they do so, neither they nor their church can justly charge discrimination if the community refuses to subsidize them in thus setting themselves apart.*

There is a new militancy against the very real issue of religious illiteracy in the land. Whatever its cause, Protestants are facing up to it unitedly—and positively. About twenty years ago, in collaboration with leading educators, they set themselves to think up ways and means of getting religion back into the schools. They came up with the "released time" plan. The movement flourished. Some three thousand

"Released time" programs provide classes in religion and religious culture, and are conducted by ministers and volunteer teachers in churches near the schools. Despite a much-misunderstood Supreme Court ruling, the project forges ahead, an admirable demonstration of church unity.

communities adopted it, with classes in religion being held either in schools or in churches. The project was, and is, an admirable demonstration of denominational unity. It worked well—until an Illinois atheist challenged the constitutionality of using the school buildings for religious classes, as in Champaign, Illinois. The "Champaign case" went to the U.S. Supreme Court; the atheist won.

Confusion, both in educational and religious circles, reigned until it became clear that the Supreme Court was not overruling the teaching of *religion* in schools. That issue had not come before any court; and if it did, no court would declare against it. True to American tradition, the court had ruled against *sectarian* teaching *on*

school property. "Released time" came back strong, once this point became clear. The program is now almost back to peak proportions, with classes being held—on "released" or "dismissed" time—in churches, in buses, in auditoriums, anywhere away from school precincts.

Protestant crusading against religious illiteracy is going further. It is now on the move to put religion back into the school curricula. Straight religion, not any form of sectarianism. And taught by school teachers, not churchmen. To any educator still chary of religion as "controversial," they are saying: So are a lot of other subjects controversial. One does not cease teaching political science because one's class contains the progeny of Democrats and Republicans, Progressives and Socialists. Nor does one exclude economics because here are the sons and daughters of free-enterprisers, social-planners and socialists. Nor does one drop literature because the community contains fanatical fans for both Shakespeare and Gertrude Stein. Nor does one scuttle art because artists have different conceptions and interpretations of religious themes.

The above is strictly in line with the opinion of Supreme Court Justice Robert H. Jackson, who, in the Champaign case, gave it this expression:

> It remains to be demonstrated whether it is possible, even if desirable, to comply with such demands as plaintiff's completely to isolate and cast out of secular education all that some people may reasonably regard as religious instruction. . . . Music without sacred music, architecture minus the cathedral, or painting without the scriptural themes would be eccentric and incomplete, even from a secular point of view. . . . Certainly a course in English literature that omitted the Bible

and other powerful uses of our mother tongue for religious ends would be pretty barren. . . . Nearly everything in our culture worth transmitting, everything which gives meaning to life, is saturated with religious influences. . . . One can hardly respect a system of education that would leave the student wholly ignorant of the currents of religious thought that move the world society for a part in which he is being prepared.

Protestants are insisting that there can be a Pedagogy of Religion just as practical as a pedagogy for any other subject. And once again the heads of Protestant groups and the heads of secular school systems are bent over a plan to give religion its rightful place, both as a separate subject in the curricula and as a contributing influence in so-called "nonreligious" courses. With assistance from men of tried faith and tested Americanism, the project now in the making promises to be such as will rescue the Christian faith from the limbo into which misguided interests and religious intolerance have forced it.

Nearly a quarter of a million public schools are spread across the country, ranging in size from one-room houses with a few pupils to commanding edifices accommodating several hundred students. All of these schools extend the privilege of free textbooks and a free education to our young people, whatever their background of race, color or creed.

IX

PROPAGATORS OF THE WORD

A propagandist, according to the dictionary-makers, is "one who propagates with zeal any doctrine, system, or principle." Great zealots, Protestants have always been great propagators. First it was the spoken word, then the printed word, now the word broadcast over the air and dramatized on the motion-picture and television screen.

As a matter of historic fact, most of the "mass communications media" which now fill the world with voices on all subjects got either their start or their most rapid development by men divinely impelled to discover faster and more effective ways of getting the Gospel to all men.

Take Martin Luther, for example. His wholesale use of Johann Gutenberg's new invention of printing got that medium off to a flying start. The indefatigable father of the Reformation was an ink-flinger of rare accomplishment. Legend has it that when Luther could not silence the Devil in any other way, he threw an ink bottle at him. Protestants have been heaving ink at Satan and all his works ever since—and with notable success.

Central in Protestantism's passion for propaganda has been the determination to get the Bible into the hands of all men everywhere—the Bible itself, not some man's or some church's interpretation of it. One of the first books to come from the Gutenberg press was the Bible. Since then many millions of copies of the Holy Scriptures, Protestantism's one and only final authority for faith and practice, have fallen like "leaves for the healing of the nations" from Protestant presses.

What that gigantic release of the Word of God has accomplished, in promoting civilization as well as piety, no man can compute. Its blasting as well as healing effects have cleansed society again and again. The bookbinder who stamped the backbone of the New Testament with the abbreviation "TNT" unwittingly labeled the contents with prophetic accuracy. Any man, however, can compute its effect on America and its establishment as a nation of free and responsible men. Our forefathers arrived with Bibles under their arms, held close to their hearts. It was the textbook of their freedom; its precepts were the foundation stones of this democracy. "The entrance of Thy Word giveth light" was Gospel to them in more ways than one.

No wonder that one of the first acts of Congress was to approve the printing of a large edition of the Bible and to recommend it to all the people. No wonder that every person taking public office, every witness in a court of law, must lay his right hand upon this final authority of all Truth. No wonder that Thomas R. Mar-

(Continued on page 152)

TOP

Pastors whose congregations are so scattered that they must be reached by plane fly over thousands of square miles to visit their charges. Like the circuit-riders of an earlier day, the modern minister uses the swiftest means to get to his people.

RIGHT

"If the people won't come to the church, take the church to the people!" That is the practice of many Protestant denominations who send their trailer chapels across the countryside in search of children and adults unreached by the Gospel.

OPPOSITE PAGE

Protestants are zealous spreaders of the Gospel, and always have been—first with the spoken word, then through printing presses, now also via radio, television and motion pictures. Besides other media, the Protestant press alone is a mighty engine for propagation of the Good News. In America today are some 950 religious journals, with a combined circulation of more than fifty million copies per issue. Most are Protestant, pouring forth a mighty tide of religious truth.

The indefatigable Dr. Billy Graham commands immense crowds wherever he makes a stand—as when he converted an Atlanta arcade stairway into an impromptu rostrum to conduct a series of daily prayer services.

TOP

Pressmen at Protestant publishing houses realize they are more than mere craftsmen; they are evangelists as well. Here the mechanical staff of one large printery pause for morning worship before setting the presses to rolling.

OPPOSITE PAGE: TOP

Evangelism at the street corner, once the exclusive preserve of the Salvation Army, is now utilized by many church and mission groups whose zeal has catapulted them from the sanctuary to the busy city intersections.

OPPOSITE PAGE: BOTTOM

Open-air evangelistic crusades are familiar crowd-stoppers in large cities of America. Christian businessmen and ministers' associations often join forces to prove that worship need not be confined to "holy places."

Journalistic schools all over the country, at the demand of young Protestants eager to specialize in religious journalism, are setting up special courses to instruct them in the special craft of using words and ideas for spiritual purposes.

The motion picture's usefulness in communicating ideas has sent Protestant churches and independent Christian laymen by the score into the production of movies for church and Sunday-school use. Hundreds of films, technically high grade and spiritually inspirational and instructional, are available as a teaching and evangelistic medium.

shall, when Vice-President, said: "If I were to have my way, I would take the torch out of the hand of the Statue of Liberty in New York harbor and, in its stead, place an open Bible."

And no wonder, either, is it that into the very early life of America there sprang up the Bible society movement with a quenchless passion to place the Bible into every hand and home in the land. Bible societies and distributing agencies are busy in every state, every city of any size. Colporteurs tirelessly rove every hinterland in America and the world. The presses of the American Bible Society, supported by fifty Protestant denominations, never stop, never turn out enough to meet the demand. In its one hundred and thirty-five years, this mighty organ for spreading the Word has distributed more than 400,000,000 Bibles or portions thereof. Laboring around the clock and around the world, its army of translators have managed for the past half-century to bring out a new translation, into a tongue hitherto without the Scriptures, once every thirty-two days. It now has the Bible printed and distributed in 1,118 languages and dialects.

Early leaders of Protestant churches were all zealous writers and publishers. John Wesley is a good example. A fabulous distributor of words himself, he inspired his preachers to write as well as speak; in early America his circuit riders crammed their saddlebags with books, which they sowed everywhere along the frontier. Wesley's Methodists in 1789 founded the Methodist Book Concern, an establishment that has flooded America and foreign lands with literature of all kinds related to the Gospel. Every other denomination likewise has its printing establishments. From them come uncounted millions of church papers, church-school literature, books, magazines, hymnals. Other millions pour from the presses of independent and undenominational publishing concerns.

Protestants get into radio and television with the speed and talent they have always devoted to the adoption of new and effective means for reaching more people. The air waves and the coaxial cables carry excellently produced religious programs into the homes of millions of nonchurchgoers. Pioneering work is carried out by the Protestant Radio Commission and Religious Television Workshop.

The first denominational paper went to press in 1789. By 1827 there were some thirty Protestant periodicals. Today in America there are no fewer than 950 religious journals representing all faiths, with a combined circulation of more than fifty million copies per issue; the overwhelming proportion of this volume is Protestant. Compare that with the sixty-five million copies per issue represented by the big "general circulation" and news magazines of America, and you get some idea of the tide of religious truth that regularly rolls over the American consciousness, teaching, guiding, inspiring.

The Protestant writer and news-gatherer, whether employed on religious or secular jour-

TOP
The widespread distribution of the Bible to homes, hotels and other places by Protestant agencies has resulted in the winning of untold numbers of individuals and families who, previous to the entrance of the light-giving Word, were apathetic to religion.

LEFT
Determined that no person doomed to physical darkness need be without spiritual light, Protestant Bible societies seized upon the Braille system and have made embossed editions of the Holy Book available to the blind.

nals, has always stood for, and fought for, "freedom of the press." Protestant editors of America's 12,000 daily and weekly newspapers, trained in the tradition of their faith, are celebrated for their refusal to wear any man's halter, their rejection of any controls, ecclesiastical or governmental, save those of their free consciences. Long before the forefathers wrote the freedom-of-the-press principle into the Constitution, there were Protestants practicing it, defending it, going to jail for it.

John Peter Zenger was one. In 1735 this editor and printer of the *Journal,* an early New York paper, was hauled into court. His offense: he had dared to expose the corruption of the Crown's governor, William Cosby. The court was packed with people, "packed" also with royalist henchmen out to see that the fearless upstart got a long prison term, perhaps even death. Then, just as it seemed the case against Zenger was all wrapped up, in came aged Andrew Hamilton, courageous Philadelphia lawyer. Angry to the core, Hamilton roasted the Governor, then turned to the jury to say: "The question before you, gentlemen, is not of small nor private concern. It is not the cause of a poor printer, not of New York alone, which you are now trying. It may in its consequence affect every free man in America. It is the cause of liberty. Every man who prefers liberty to a life of slavery will bless and honor you as men who have baffled an attempt of tyranny and, by an impartial verdict, have laid the foundation for securing for ourselves, our posterity and our neighbors that to which Nature and the laws have given us a right: the liberty both of exposing and opposing arbitrary power and by speaking and writing Truth!"

Purple went the faces of the Governor's henchmen, and angry was the voice of the Chief Justice as he virtually instructed the jury to bring in a verdict against Zenger. But the

Among the truly great but humble missionaries of the Word are the Bible colporteurs who constantly rove the isolated and back-country sections of America to put the Book of Books into the hands of otherwise neglected and unchurched people.

jury, free citizens all, came back with the shout: "Not guilty!" And cheers rocked the room.

Hamilton's speech went all over the colonies. It won one of our first major battles for press freedom. Today, more than two hundred years later, it comes down to us in the Bill of Rights and the rumble of every free press in the land. Hearing that voice and that rumble are 150,-000,000 Americans, who, as readers of American magazines and papers almost without number, are the freest and best informed people in the world.

Quick to seize upon printing as a means to spread the Gospel, Protestants have been

For more than half a century the tireless Gideons, one of the oldest of interdenominational evangelistic associations, have been putting Bibles within reach of travelers, hospital patients, public school students and members of the armed forces. Directed by Christian businessmen, the association seldom misses an opportunity to dramatize its effective distribution of the Word.

equally quick to adopt other and more up-to-date means. Protestantism got into radio and television with the speed and vision it has always manifested toward any new medium for reaching more people. Radio was scarcely born before religion was called in to rock the cradle. The first national hookup for religion was given the newly formed National Radio Pulpit, with Dr. S. Parkes Cadman preaching. Dr. Daniel A. Poling soon followed with his immensely popular National Youth Radio Conference; by 1936

it was declared the widest-heard religious program on the air.

The Protestant Radio Commission, comprised of twenty-four church and interchurch agencies, today assists the networks with such broadcasts as the "National Radio Pulpit," the "Art of Living," "National Vespers," "Gems for Thought," "Faith in Our Times" and "Morning Chapel." Besides the direct network programs, the Commission produces many transcribed "platters" for local station use; the

As a technique for ensnaring the interest of un-churched youth as well as for more effective teaching in Sunday schools, the motion picture has proved ideal for propagating the Word in entertaining and dramatic fashion. The production of more and better audio-visual tools for church use promises to revitalize Protestantism's historic passion for evangelization as well as education.

"Radio Edition of the Bible" and the children's program "All Aboard for Adventure" are but two. Now deep in television, the Commission is putting on the air religious films, Bible puppet shows, and such general interest features as "The Meeting House," designed to depict entertainingly as well as dramatically the place of the church in the community. In addition, the Commission regularly conducts a series of institutes and workshops which train local religious leaders in the complex and highly specialized use of radio and television techniques.

Other Protestant programs are on the networks too, and with audiences whose size and responsiveness make commercial sponsors covetous. Of top listener interest for many years have been "The Lutheran Hour," founded by the late Dr. Walter A. Maier, and Dr. Charles E. Fuller's "Old-Fashioned Revival Hour"; both hit the air waves with music and a message hewing straight to the Gospel line, and each has a worshiping congregation of more than twenty

HOLINESS TO THE LORD

SO BE YE HOLY

Great camp meetings and summer assemblies, such as this one at Ocean Grove, N. J., enable zealous Protestants to reach far beyond the confines of the usual Christian fold to attract vacationing Americans at a period when leisure hours give them time to ponder the Christian Gospel.

million listeners. Another twenty million are claimed for Dr. Billy Graham's "Hour of Decision."

In addition to the big network programs, there are many hundreds of others of local derivation. A full 90 per cent of American communities with councils of churches, as well as many individual Protestant church groups, regularly take to the air with worship services, religious news broadcasts, hymn sings, "town meeting" discussions of religion and its importance to American life.

With a deep-down conviction that religion is needed today more than ever, some top-grade business and industrial leaders, who are also devoted Protestant laymen, have overruled their more crass associates to insist that their radio money be spent for programs of spiritual message. The result: such inspirational offerings as "Hymns of All Churches," "The Light of the World" and "The Greatest Story Ever Told." Opera and concert singers and orchestra leaders such as Phil Spitalny and Fred Waring confess that their programs get the biggest listener reaction when the old Gospel hymns are rendered. And "America's Town Meeting of the Air," founded and directed by George V. Denny, Jr., is as Protestant in its approach to free discussion as it is true to the American principle of "hear both sides and make up your own mind."

The motion picture is another medium Protestants have adopted with vision and vigor. They have both influenced the Hollywood products, far more than is generally known, and have plunged into the production business themselves, to supply films for religious education. So far as the first is concerned, it must be admitted that Hollywood had them fretful for years. Not having any united voice, Protestantism worried long over the deleterious effect the movies were having on morals; the protests of its separate pulpits and conclaves went unheeded. In the field already was the Roman Catholic Legion of Decency, which sedulously protected its own rights in Hollywood with a pressure both heavy and effective. Protestants, however, often saw their clergy lampooned, their standards of moral purity flouted. While militant lobbyists from almost every other field were entrenched in the motion-picture capital to see that their interests were favorably treated, Protestantism has no stick to hold over producers. The situation finally reached the point that, as one producer quipped: "The only fellow you can make into a villain these days is a native white Protestant!"

Then, characteristically, Protestants broke out in an indignant storm that threatened to engulf the motion-picture industry with disaster. The net result was the formation of the Protestant Motion Picture Council. No pressure group with selfish intent, the PMPC went into action to clean up the films for everybody, not just Protestants. And instead of adopting a completely negative approach, it took the typically Protestant positive route. Its objective reviews of current films, written by experts of proven ability and concern for religion and morality, are released to hundreds of newspapers and magazines monthly. Its personnel are regularly consulted by the industry in the endeavor to avoid Protestant displeasure. Entertainment motion pictures may still be far from

To bring the Christian faith graphically to the attention of all Americans is ever a matter of active concern to Protestants. In the above case, artful laymen of a Los Angeles rescue mission put across the point with a beautiful float made of varicolored chrysanthemums entered in Pasadena's Tournament of Roses parade.

ideal fare. But there has been improvement. And a great deal of the credit must be chalked up to the PMPC's endless appeal to producers to make their product more consonant with Christian ideals.

The motion picture's usefulness in communicating ideas has sent Protestant churches by the score and independents by the hundreds into the business of producing movies for church and church-school use. There is no field of communications more active. Audio-visual tools— for teaching the Bible, the principles of brotherhood, the Christian way of life—are coming forth in staggering numbers. So staggering, indeed, that the churches' teaching systems have not yet caught up with them. But they are catching up fast. Working with the interdenominational agencies for religious education is the Protestant Film Commission. The PFC is in the producing business itself, having brought out a long list of high-quality films geared closely to study and mission themes.

Also in the business of propagating the Gospel story, both in church and in unchurched highways and hedges of American life, are posters, billboards, window and streetcar cards, slides and filmstrips, phonograph recordings, public-address systems and all the hundred and one different gadgets modern man uses to capture the ear and eye of the public.

From Martin Luther and his early Protestants, laboring against great handicaps to get the Gospel out to the people via block type and rough paper, to today's churchmen and their multifarious uses of modern communications may seem like a far cry. But the same spirit obtains. The Gospel must be spread, and quickly. And it is the *Gospel* Protestants are concerned with, not Protestantism itself. Protestants shape their powerful propaganda to win men to Christ—period. Than that, there is no higher or nobler propaganda. And none, it seems when you assess the ever-mounting power of the churches, is more effective!

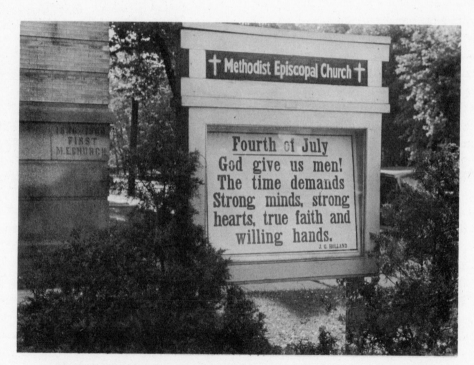

Church bulletin boards, often called "wayside pulpits," do their part to proclaim to the casual passerby a summons to active Christian citizenship.

X

WORLD OUTREACH

All the evidence seems to indicate that when God touches a Protestant's soul, He puts a map in his hand and a word in his heart. The map is a *world* map, and the word is one-syllabled: *Go!* "Go teach . . . Go preach . . . Go tell of Me . . . Go into all the world, to every living creature." Go, go, go! And under that divine imperative, how these Protestants have gone!

In the nineteen hundred years since the Master laid that imperative on the hearts of a handful of humble men in an obscure pocket of the world, Christianity has girdled the globe, gathered to itself a constituency of more than 600,000,000 persons of every race and color on earth. Of that total, the Protestant churches —younger by several hundreds of years than either of Christendom's two other major divisions: Eastern Orthodox and Roman Catholic —have a sizable proportion.

The Protestant has always been marked as a spiritual adventurer. Like Paul the Apostle, his ears have always been tuned for Macedonian calls, his feet eager to obey that injunction, "Go!" That has been especially true of Anglo-Saxon Protestants, who have been responsible for a full seven-eighths of the Protestant world mission. From Britain and America, during the past century and a half, has flowed a thrilling tide of men and women into every non-Christian land, eager to cast their light into superstition's darkness, eager to burn themselves out for Christ.

William Carey heard the far bugles calling while at his cobbler's bench in England, and he closed his shop door forever that he might open the Gospel door to India. David Livingstone heard the bugles while tending a spinning jenny; they pulled him to his feet and projected him into the depths of darkest Africa. Robert Morrison heard them while peering at a map of the Orient in his study, and was immediately off to traipse the China hinterland and bring a Christian literature to a million peasants. Adoniram Judson heard them while reading a sermon entitled "The Star of the East," and he soon was burning up a hundred Burma roads with the Gospel torch. John G. Paton heard them while roving the pleasant pastures of his native Scotch highlands, and promptly set sail for the turbulent tropics and the New Hebrides.

These are but five of a number that is legion. You can call the roll of the intrepid pioneers for hours and never exhaust the list. Some lighted out for the distant horizons with only the Bible under their arms and a call to preach in their hearts; some with medical kits and lancets in hand; some with tools over their shoulders and bags of improved seeds in their pockets; some with degrees in pedagogy or medicine or agriculture or divinity; some with

More than any other people on earth, Americans tend to look toward the far horizons. That trait, arising from a pioneering heritage and allied with an evangelizing imperative, brought our Protestant forefathers to America in the first place. It has been responsible for girdling of the globe with an immense missionary program—evangelical, medical, agricultural and educational—that is the amazement of the modern world, and is now seen by civil and church leaders alike as our best hope in the war against Communism and all other atheistic and inhuman ideologies.

nothing save a spirit burning to "further the Gospel" merely by living with and humbly serving the people. But whyever and wherever they went, they left footprints as long as the stride of God.

Is it statistics you want? Then glance at these: Today in so-called "non-Christian" lands, Protestantism has more than 6,000 mission centers in a hundred countries. This does not include the many thousands of independent preaching stations and other small but restricted missions. A "mission center" is far more than just a church; it is an organized unit for a considerable area. Connected with these centers are more than 55,000 churches; 57,000 schools and colleges; 62,000 Sunday schools; 3,500 hospitals and dispensaries—to say nothing of leprosariums, orphanages, agricultural institutes, publishing houses and other agencies almost without number. Staffing the centers are

Missionaries in Japan, one of the few remaining nations of the Orient where the doors are open to unrestricted Christian enterprise, are currently facing one of the greatest opportunities for Protestant expansion among a people eager for both Christianity and democracy. Protestant churches and schools are crowded, with missionaries and teachers in great demand and short supply.

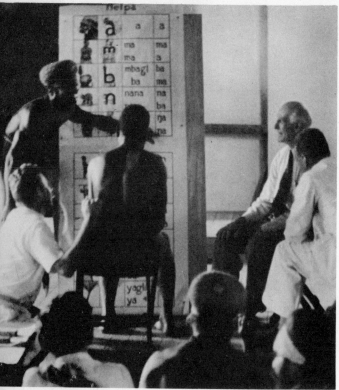

25,000 ordained ministers, native and foreign; 100,000 native teachers; 20,000 doctors and nurses; and 100,000 other full-time workers.

More than a half of this total enterprise of world Protestantism is manned by missionaries and workers from America; a full two-thirds of it is financed by American dollars. At the peak of the foreign missionary effort, prior to World War II, there were 14,000 American missionaries abroad; behind them were millions of Protestant laymen and thousands of mission societies who built up an annual missions war chest in excess of forty million dollars.

Americans more than any other people, and out of all proportion to their numerical strength, have been missionary-minded. That mission-mindedness is part and parcel of their pioneering heritage. The American Protestant takes to the frontier, wherever it is, with the habitual drift of a man gravitating to his natural environment. It was the missionary impulse, in large part, that brought the colonists to America in the first place. Both the 1606 and 1609 Virginia charters made plain that one of the chief

TOP LEFT
The outreach of Protestant denominations has brought about vital changes in every land penetrated—not only in the lifting of the people spiritually but in the establishment of educational and health projects. Nowhere is this change better evidenced than in Latin America, where Protestants must battle against deep-rooted religious superstition and clerical-incited opposition.

BOTTOM LEFT
One of the most significant works of the Protestant foreign missions program is its immensely important drive to stamp out illiteracy among the one billion people in the world who can neither read nor write—nor, therefore, vote. Leader of the Protestant literacy army is Dr. Frank Laubach whose "Each one teach one" project causes present governments to clamor for his services.

Bible classes are held in the jungles of Asia and Africa, where native teachers, converted and educated by Protestant missionaries, instruct their people in Christianity and also give them vocational training to lift their economic standing and improve their social conditions. Teachers received their training in mission schools built by American churches in every mission land.

reasons for settling these shores was the propagation of the Christian faith. That impulse put Protestants in the van of every wagon train off to the westward-moving frontiers, sent them out to meet immigrants, induced them to build churches and schools in immigrant settlements, in big cities and on prairies, in mining towns and lumber camps. For a century and a half, they did not go abroad; their focus was held to the new continent. There was plenty to keep them busy.

The Indians occupied their first missionary zeal. Many of the early colonists, like Roger Williams and William Penn, fought for fair treatment for the Indians, fought to a standstill the crasser elements who would rob the red man of everything but his breechcloth. Missionaries sought them out; churches and schools were built for them. Dartmouth College, begun on what was then the frontier, was founded primarily to train missionaries in the art of winning Indians to Christ. Harvard's charter dedicated it to "the education of the English and Indian youth in knowledge and godlynes."

Negroes were American Protestantism's next concern. Whether in North or South, Protestants were first to develop a conscience about the black man and his lot. First through emancipation and then through education, they struck off his chains. Practically all the secondary and higher schools for Negroes were established by Protestants; even today their top colleges and universities are Protestant in origin. No wonder that historians such as Kenneth Scott Latourette can say: "The American Negro mind is to a considerable degree the creation of

During its 135 years the American Bible Society, through the labors of missionaries and colporteurs, has distributed four hundred million copies of the Word across the world.

Christian missions." To the Protestant doctrine of the inherent dignity of man, his right to regard himself as a child of God without reference to the color of his skin, the Negro responded as he has responded to no other faith. Today the overwhelming majority of Negroes who are Christians are also Protestant; mostly Baptists and Methodists.

With equal missionary purpose, Protestants went to the Orientals who had settled thickly on the West Coast. Though of later vintage, this mission's enterprise is significant. By the start of World War II, Protestantism had become the prevailing Christian faith among Chinese and Japanese. And to Protestantism the Nisei,

American-born of Japanese parentage, credit a good part of their Americanization as well as their Christianization. After Pearl Harbor, during one of the most trying sets of circumstances ever foisted upon a people of foreign parentage, the Nisei proved themselves loyal to both faith and country. When the furore of resettlement broke out on the Coast, with chauvinistic groups yelling for Nisei hides, the Protestant churches were virtually the only sizable force which went to bat for the Japanese-Americans, shaming the land for the legal and social discriminations being practiced against them. The Nisei haven't forgotten that!

It was early in the nineteenth century that American Protestants began to focus their eyes on the far frontiers. While still hurling the tentacles of their faith into every area of American life in need of evangelization, they began reaching out to other lands. Lovers of all that Protestantism had developed in their homeland, they craved to export its boons abroad. There is nothing incongruous in the fact that the Baptist clergyman who wrote the hymn "America" in his student days later became secretary of his denomination's foreign missionary society. Church historians call the period 1815-1914 "The Great Century," the epoch of Protestantism's greatest expansion.

Out they went—to India and Africa, whose immensely rich resources had for centuries tempted foreign plunderers; out to lands where the bodies of animals were sacred and men's bodies cheap, where gods were wood and stone, and where misery rode the back and poverty ached in the stomach and hopelessness cried in the heart; out to China and Burma and Malaya and the islands of the sea; out to the outcaste, the untouchable, the diseased, the blighted. Almost every local church formed its missionary society. Pennies and dimes and dollars began dropping into missionary boxes; clothing and food and books into missionary barrels. Denominational leaders got out their big maps, began to plan world strategy. The Student Volunteer Movement wrote on its banner: "The evangelism of the world in this generation!" and enrolled tens of thousands of young Protestants for foreign service. Individual Christians hearkened to their hearts and began to hear God's word saying: "Go!"

Out they went and out they continued to go—right up to the eve of Pearl Harbor. World War II temporarily halted the march, but it brought to blazing light what had been happening in the world's far corners whence those immigrants for Christ had gone. American GI's, fanning out all over the world, found some amazing Christians in some amazing places. Back from the war fronts, they sent letters to loved ones telling tales that seemed tall even to supporters of foreign missions. Their lives had been saved by mission-converted ex-cannibals. Their broken and fever-ridden bodies had been transported over the Owen Stanley ranges by "fuzzywuzzy" stretcher-bearers with "a look on their faces that makes you think that Christ was black." They had been fished out of the sea, spirited to safety, nursed to health and returned to their comrades by natives who couldn't speak their language but could sing their Protestant hymn tunes. Following the blazing path of war, they had come upon Christian communities distinguished by a character of life sharply contrasting with the life around them, had met everywhere Bible-carrying and hymn-singing Christians of varied hues where atlases and military intelligence had indicated only savages.

The war revised a lot of things for the men and women of our armed forces. Not least of **the** revisions was the popular conception of the missionary. When one thought of a missionary, he conjured up a cartoonist's caricature. Per-

American and native translators connected with the American Bible Society have made the Holy Scriptures available in some 1,118 languages to virtually every non-Christian land.

haps it was of a dried-up spinster, taking her maladjustment and frustrations to a people naïve and uninhibited, forcing their bodies into Mother Hubbards and their minds into straitjackets. Or perhaps it was of a stringy and hawk-nosed killjoy, forever thrusting a Bible under a cultured Hindu or Chinese nose and insisting that he flee his heathen beliefs and hasten to the mourner's bench. Instead of this caricature, the war uncovered great Protestant scholars, medical and natural scientists, educators.

The GI's ran into men of the stature of Albert Schweitzer, one of the towering figures of our times, or any times, a man of tremendously

In countries of non-Christian basic culture, such as Japan, high schools and colleges are maintained by American Protestant denominations to educate youth in the Christian ethic and spirit. In Hindu and Islamic countries also, American schools of higher learning graduate hundreds who go on to occupy positions of high professional and governmental leadership, to the benefit of their countries.

varied talents, content to lose himself in the lives of Africa's black men. They saw men like Sam Higgenbottom, who has brought to India his immense achievements in Christian agriculture, and Emory Alvord who in thirty years has changed the face of Southern Rhodesia by the application of his "Gospel of the Plow." They came upon the monuments of Christian healing left by great medical missionaries like Gordon Seagrave, "Burma Surgeon," whose triumphs over disease were such as to make Hippocrates rise from his Grecian grave and applaud. They followed hard upon the trail of men like globe-girdling Frank Laubach who, with his "Each one teach one" program, is generalissimo in the world crusade to stamp out illiteracy among the one billion citizens on this planet who can neither read nor write—nor, therefore, vote.

The revelation was not alone to servicemen. Franklin D. Roosevelt wrote before his death: "Since becoming President, I have come to know that the finest type of Americans we have abroad are the missionaries of the Cross. I am humiliated that I am just finding out at this late day the work of foreign missions and the nobility of the missionary." Wendell Willkie

American Protestantism for almost a century has been exporting our brand of education and a "reservoir of good will" to mission countries, as in this native school in Guatemala. The Protestant drive against ignorance and superstition embraces some 57,000 such schools around the earth—all begun and many still supported by consecrated vision and dedicated dollars.

went junketing around the earth during the war, and came back to tell of the great "reservoir of good will" America has in foreign lands, thanks in large part to missionary enterprise, and to abandon isolationism forever and become the foremost spokesman for the "One World" ideal.

The Protestant foreign missions enterprise had long been laying the foundations for one world. To begin with, it had been mainly responsible for world Protestant unity. Because sectarian divisiveness simply could not stand when pitted against hostile and pagan cultures, the missionary churches had to join hands. Missions administrators at home were constrained to follow. As early as 1854, the denominations' missions boards were getting together to eliminate duplication, rule out overlapping. Large missionary conferences followed, and with each there was more and more talk between delegates of bigger and better co-operation. And if abroad, why not at home?

Prominent at all these conferences were delegates from the mission fields—not missionaries only but an ever-increasing number of indigenous leaders. With the rise of native leader-

American women missionaries are specialists in many fields, practicing medicine, nursing the sick, teaching agriculture and handcraft, training youth and the illiterate. Whether in lonely outposts of America or in infested African villages, they are the heroines of God's army.

ship, the "mission churches" dropped that term; they became the "Younger Churches." Right there, incidentally, is a sharp and significant difference between Protestant and other missionary enterprise. Especially in the last half-century, Protestantism has followed the same policy with its mission churches that America has followed with its dependencies—the Philippines, for example. It has educated these churches for self-determination, raised up native leaders for self-supporting independence. American Protestants, above all others, can understand this yearning by the humbler peoples for independence; they have fostered it, geared their future programs toward it. Thus hundreds upon hundreds of mission churches, now under their own leaders, have shed the "missionary" appellation and have joined the growing number of Younger Churches.

Strangely enough—or is it strange?—the world demand for Protestant unity grew in direct ratio to the rise of the self-determining Younger Churches. This demand was amplified and made challenging by such successful experiments in unity as the International Missionary Conference, the Foreign Missions Conference of North America, the Missionary Education Movement. Out of every conclave came committees appointed to explore bases for broader co-operation.

Protestant world unity was a mammoth ideal on the march. Nothing could stop it. Champions of interchurch understanding arose in every denomination. One of the greatest and most durable was Episcopal Bishop Charles H. Brent. At a world-wide missionary conference in Edinburgh in 1910, the good bishop threw out the challenge: "The world is too strong for a divided Church!" His vision was resoundingly reflected by such other mighty prophets as William Temple, later Archbishop of Canterbury—and the ecumenical flame was lighted.

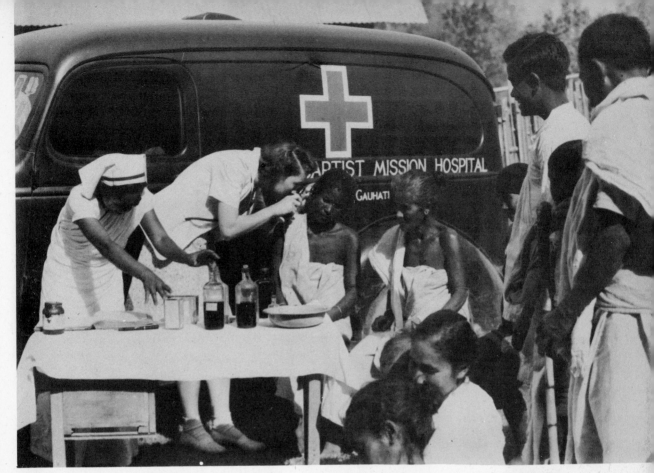

To tiny villages in the back country, whose people often never before had seen any doctor or received medical treatment other than by witch doctors, go "hospitals on wheels" equipped with medical supplies and skilled physicians supplied by American Protestant mission boards.

Here at Edinburgh was inaugurated the Faith and Order Movement, chief carrier of the fire destined to burn from Protestantism all the dross of divisiveness.

Other great conferences were held—at Stockholm in 1925, Lausanne in 1927, Jerusalem in 1928, Oxford in 1937. Then in 1938, at Utrecht, came the historic decision to get going, without further delay, on a plan for world federation of all non-Roman church bodies. (The Roman church was invited, but declined—unless all Protestants were prepared to "return to Mother Church.")

It was a big order, this demand for the World Council of Churches. But it was a Christian imperative. It didn't come about at once; another world war intervened. Yet, on the job provisionally, the incipient World Council proved itself. While nations were gnashing at each other, and the rest of the world was splitting apart, the Council kept Christians together right across the war's lines. It promoted an international service to chaplains, an elaborate system of aid to prisoners and refugees, carried on relief and reconstruction, employed the underground to keep Christian leaders of

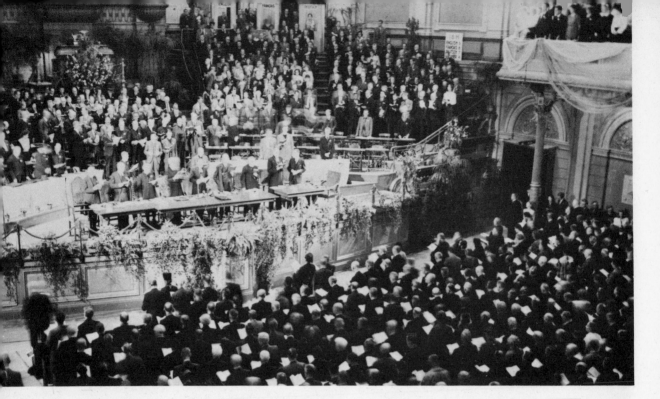

The ideal of Protestant world unity for international action bore its greatest fruit in the formation in 1948 of the World Council of Churches. This brought into close communion one hundred fifty million Christians of one hundred and fifty denominations in 44 countries across the world.

warring nations in touch with one another. Before the blustering might of "master men," Protestants of all nations stood true to the Master of men. Once again, in mysterious ways the infinite God proved how He can make even the wrath of men to praise Him, how man's most evil instrument—war—can be used to work His holiest designs.

In 1948 the World Council came into official being with its first assembly at Amsterdam. Ten years had gone into its prayerful construction, ten of the most eventful years in human history. What eventuated was perhaps the most important and enheartening event since the Reformation. Into the Council came 150,000,000 Christians, representing 156 denominations from 44 countries. No mere gathering of ecclesiastical globe-trotters, the assembly drew Protestants from the far ends of the earth—not only to sign on the dotted line for their churches, but to discuss "Man's Disorder and God's Design." The assembly message was highhearted and firm-lipped:

Christ has made us His own, and He is not divided. In seeking Him, we find one another. Here at Amsterdam we have committed ourselves afresh to Him, and have covenant with one another in constituting this World Council of Churches. We intend to stay together.

You can thank foreign missions for that achievement in Protestant union! You can thank them for much more. Missions have, all through the long years, done an educational job on Americans that is deeply significant today. Long before isolationists countered globality by calling it "globaloney," missions have taught us to think in global terms. Missionaries through the years have kept America's mind keyed to the

The Protestant foreign missions enterprise has, throughout the long years, done more than bring Christian civilization to foreign lands. It has performed also an educational job on Americans, whose investment of interest and money in such enterprise has taught them to think and act brotherly with peoples of the whole wide world. The spirit of world friendship inevitably is the basic Christian virtue which finally will pyramid into a just and lasting peace among the world's peoples.

fact that peoples beyond the seas and beyond our ken were important. More, they have taught Americans to think *brotherly*—to think about the world's peoples in a way that had nothing to do with commercial or political exploitation.

What this has meant, and will mean in the future, nobody can possibly assess. But one would be both unfair and unrealistic if, in auditing the reasons for America's growth from fierce isolationism into world responsibility, he did not ring with red pencil those long years when Protestants have been preaching the infinite worth of every man, irrespective of color or race, and when Protestants by the millions have been acquiring a universal sympathy, a universal conscience, through their interest in and support of world-wide missions.

"AN IDEA WHOSE TIME HAS COME"

America, we started out by saying, began with the Big Idea that man, made in God's own image, can and must be free. In our swift panorama we have seen how that idea, the very genius of the Judeo-Christian tradition, was implanted and preserved in the hearts of men for centuries, and how eventually it was brought to these shores by our Protestant forefathers, cradled here, nurtured here, matured here. We have seen how it has been so woven into the warp and woof of American life that it is the explanation and the glory of all this country is and hopes to be.

Let us face it: America is not perfect. Our way of life has its alleys down which we hate to look. There is still corruption, injustice, inequity; the Big Idea has not performed its work completely. Nor are Protestants perfect; let us face that too. Their weaknesses have been the weaknesses of any people failing with tragic incongruity to live up always to their highest and best. They have done things they ought not to have done, left undone those things they should have done. The fact that Protestants frankly admit their failures, and are at work to correct them—that is the surest and best guarantee of their eventual "going on toward perfection." Briefly, let us look at some of these weaknesses:

Too many Protestants, laity and clergy alike, have stultified the Protestant ideal with sectarian pride and self-interest. They have had their periods of isolationist lethargy, been divided when they should have been united, local-minded when they should have been world-minded. In the past, and occasionally in very recent years, they have given false dignity to their divisions, perpetuating concepts of "distinctive differences" which, though once important, are of little value in a modern world contemptuous of sectarianism. With horizons too often limited to local church or denomination, they have thought of themselves as Methodists and Lutherans and Baptists and Presbyterians and Episcopalians when they should have been thinking and acting as members of the great Body of Christ.

It is a charge, too sadly founded on fact, that some Protestant churches have been guilty of a kind of middle-class smugness that has made the stranger and the poor feel unwelcome and unwanted. Individual congregations have been too slow to reach out to the unchurched, especially to those of an economic or social class below or above their own. This has driven a great many of the unsought into strange cults, into the hands of fanatical purveyors of weird doctrines, or, worse still, into secularity and indifference.

In many communities Protestants have been

tardy in the employment of their powers, unitedly, in the expression of common goals; on important matters of community interest, the voice of Protestantism often has been indistinct simply because it was so various.

Above all, Protestants have been too ignorant of the glories of their historic faith and too indifferent toward its tremendous importance as the savior of a civilization rocked with forces out to destroy it. Too many have been "victimized by a false tolerance," as Charles Clayton Morrison puts it, "that has enervated Protestantism's sense of mission and caused their own faith to be watered down into humanitarianism and sentimentalism."

Yet for all these and other ways in which Protestants have failed Protestantism, this faith, as we have seen in the foregoing chapters, has done more to better the lot of mankind and to design the shape of things to come than has any evangelical movement in human history. Youngest of all the world's major faiths, so far as its institutional expression is concerned, it is the most virile on earth today. That virility is intimately related to the yeasty rise in this modern world of what we have been calling the Big Idea of freedom.

Protestantism has been inevitably cast for its role as chief adversary of Communism. For it has been Protestantism in the main which first unleashed the ideal of freedom and set it singing in the hearts of men. Protestantism has endowed all humankind with what *Fortune* magazine, in its February, 1951, issue, called "the Permanent Revolution . . . the revolution of the human individual against all forms of enslavement; against all forms of earthly power, whether spiritual, political or economic, that seek to govern man without consulting his individual will."

Communist propaganda could make a good case from that. The "incriminating evidence" is all there: this faith took the lead in propagating notions about the dignity and value of the individual, about human rights and liberties being God-given to all. It built, in all its "misguided zeal," a model of democracy where all men have freedom to live and work and believe as they choose, and where the state is the servant and not the master of the people. Then it exported these "subversive ideas" about the world and, in a form of devastating germ warfare, sowed them into the minds of bondaged people everywhere. No wonder that the enslaved and ignorant little people in every land are arising to make trouble for their masters. And no wonder that Soviet Communism must react violently to "save the world from the freedom-mongers"; it must guide the world's peoples—gently if possible, forcibly if necessary—back to their comfortable slavery.

Soviet Russia and her satellites know their real enemy. They freely acknowledge that the greatest barriers to the Kremlin's dream of world domination are the freedom-loving Protestant countries. Peoples long trained in the acceptance of authoritarian control, whether temporal or spiritual, become relatively easy conquests for Communism. Peoples schooled in the concept of religious and political liberty are harder to handle. In a recent issue of *Look* magazine, Bishop G. Bromley Oxnam wrote:

Communism has not made headway in Protestant Finland, Protestant Sweden, Protestant Norway, Protestant Denmark, Protestant Holland or Protestant Great Britain. On the other hand, Italy, which is 99 per cent Roman Catholic, was but recently in danger of Communist revolution. Poland, Czechoslovakia, Hungary and Austria are in the Moscow orbit, and France has been seriously infiltrated. Catholic Spain is free from Communism, but only at the cost of a bloody civil war and a Fascist dictatorship. Today, Protestant Australia and Protestant New Zealand are not threatened by Communism. Protestant United

States is in no serious danger of accepting Communism—certainly not in the great rural areas which are overwhelmingly Protestant, nor in the Protestant West with its heritage of the individualistic pioneer and the itinerant preacher, nor in the Protestant South. It is high time that Protestant strength and Protestant strategy be understood.

Nowhere has Protestant strength and strategy been more skillfully applied recently than in the realm of international statecraft. Long before the end of World War II, the Protestant churches, through such high-level instruments as the Federal Council's Department of International Justice and Goodwill and its Commission on a Just and Durable Peace, were making the mind of Christianity known to all the nations. In 1946 the World Council of Churches formed its powerful Commission of the Churches on International Affairs, with Dr. O. Frederick Nolde as director. The contribution toward world order by these and similar Protestant agencies has been incalculable.

Any roll call of statesmen who have had an important part in founding and preserving the United Nations is heavy with the names of Protestants, from the United States and other preponderantly Protestant countries and from far lands touched by the foreign missions enterprise. While those of other faiths and backgrounds have had their part in this great organized endeavor to bring peace and brotherhood to earth, one is not surprised to find that the most dedicated battlers in the United Nations rally behind the leadership of well-known, distinguished and militant Protestants who, as delegates to the UN from America and abroad, keep the free nations ever fighting to preserve their own freedom and to make the same available to enchained people everywhere.

Nor should anyone be surprised that when a "Universal Declaration of Human Rights" was adopted by the United Nations in December, 1948, this lofty document was largely authored, sponsored and piloted through the General Assembly by these and other Protestants. The Declaration is recommended reading; it marks an epoch in human aspirations. And should anyone doubt its American Protestant tone and timber, he would do well first to reread the Constitution of the United States and the Bill of Rights, then turn to the United Nations' pronouncement and hear there such unmistakable echoes of Early American Protestant sentiments as these in Articles 1 and 18:

All human beings are born free and equal in dignity and rights. They are endowed with reason and conscience and should act towards one another in a spirit of brotherhood. . . . Everyone has the right to freedom of thought, conscience and religion; this right includes freedom to change his religion or belief, and freedom either alone or in community with others, and in public or private, to manifest his religion or belief in teaching, practice, worship and observance.

It is obvious that the great freedom ideal has made far strides into the heart of mankind since the "stern impassioned stress" of Pilgrim feet "a thoroughfare for freedom beat across the wilderness." It is even more obvious that Protestantism, prime extender of that thoroughfare across the world wilderness, confronts today a challenge of heroic proportions.

"Nothing in this world," said Victor Hugo, "is so powerful as an idea whose time has come." Can anyone, facing the tremendous upsurge of the world's peoples toward religious, social and political liberty doubt that the time of the Big Idea has come?

One stupendous fact comes down to us from mankind's long struggle upward: though political systems may come and go, faiths wax and wane, only that system and that faith which has liberty at its heart will stand. *The future is forever with the free!*

ACKNOWLEDGMENTS

Upon completion of this book it is gratifying to pay tribute and express gratitude to the many clergymen and church officers who have encouraged the authors and benefited them with their kind co-operation. Together with skillful camera artists they have graciously contributed penetrating and eloquent illustrations to the imposing pictorial study of American Protestantism. This composite picture of spiritual concern and human endeavor has grown out of the religious life of Protestants and of the everyday activities in their churches. In the panoramic view they appear in fullness and with reality as life itself has produced them, and as history records the various aspects of a dynamic religious movement.

For the pictures (Numerals refer to Pages) sincere thanks are given and credit is due to:

American Baptist Convention 57, 164

American Baptist Home Mission Society 38, 45

American Bible Society 154, 155, 166, 167

American Friends Service Committee 67, 87

Baptist Board of Education—Paul C. Carter 54, 65, 85, 143

Bell and Howell Co. 157

Bettmann Archive 10, 11, 12, 16, 17, 132, 135

Broadway Tabernacle Congregational Church —Robert L. Warne 55, 67

Brown Brothers 17

Cathedral Films 152

Cathedral of St. John the Divine 35

Christian Endeavor Society 89

Christian Herald 113, 148

Church Federation, Dayton, Ohio 144, 145

Church World Service 118

City of New York—Board of Education 126, 128, 129, 130, 133, 135

Cleveland Church Federation 101

Columbia University 139

Committee on World Literacy and Christian Literature 164

Congregational Christian Churches, Board of Foreign Missions 163, 168

CROP 120

Crusader Magazine 110, 150, 171

Culver Service 15, 19

Evangelical and Reformed Church 42

Federal Council of the Churches of Christ in America 104

Foreign Missions Council 170

The Gideon 156

Harvard University 136

Home Missions Council 116, 117

Library of Congress 95, 161

The Lutheran 36, 43, 50, 51

Lutheran Church—Missouri Synod 80

Madison Avenue Presbyterian Church —John T. Hoffmann 54

Mennonite Central Committee 118

Methodist Information 38, 44, 51, 52, 56, 57, 59, 61, 62, 77, 78, 79, 87, 105, 110, 112, 162

National Council of the Churches of Christ in the U. S. A. 90

National Council of Protestant Episcopal Churches 33, 39, 60, 66, 80, 149

National Council of the Young Men's Christian Association 86

National Lutheran Council 85, 149, 172

New York City Mission Society 82, 83, 84

Noroton Presbyterian Church —Rev. Lawrence MacCall Horton 41

Ocean Grove Camp Association 158

Presbyterian Church in the U. S. A.—Board of
    Foreign Missions 169
Presbyterian Church in the U. S. A.—Board of
    National Missions; Frederick R. Thorne
    116, 117
Presbyterian Life 81, 96
Princeton University 137
Protestant Radio Commission 153
Religious News Service 26, 48, 77, 99, 100,
    102, 108, 111, 118, 123, 124, 159
Riverside Church—Lilo Kaskell 66
Salvation Army 114, 115, 150
Seamen's Church Institute of New York 113
Seventh-Day Adventist Press Bureau 32, 69,
    151, 165
Sons of the Revolution 16

Southern Baptist Sunday School Board 68,
    154
Standard Oil Co. 64, 65, 92, 112
Syracuse University School of Journalism 151
Union Theological Seminary 59, 74
United Church Canvass 58
United Church Women 70, 71, 72
University of Pennsylvania 140
U. S. Army 47
U. S. Navy 46
Wilson, Kenneth L. 24, 25, 28
Woman's American Baptist Home Mission
    Society 69, 122
World Friendship Among Children 121, 173
Yale University 142
Youth for Christ International 88

Photos by Holisher *7, 8, 13, 21, 22, 27, 29, 30, 31, 32, 78, 79, 80, 93, 94, 96, 98, 99, 138*

BIBLIOGRAPHY

Acton, Lord, *Essays on Freedom and Power;* Beacon Press, 1948.

Blanshard, Paul, *American Freedom and Catholic Power;* Beacon Press, 1949.

Blau, Joseph L., *Cornerstones of Religious Freedom in America;* Beacon Press, 1949.

Burns, J. A., *The Growth and Development of the Catholic School System in the United States;* Benzinger, 1912.

Butts, Freeman, *The American Tradition in Religion and Education;* Beacon Press, 1950.

Clark, Elmer T., *The Small Sects in America;* Abingdon-Cokesbury, 1949.

Comfort, William Wistar, *Quakers in the Modern World;* Macmillan, 1949.

Commons, John R., *Races and Immigrants in America;* Macmillan, 1920.

Dexter, Elizabeth Anthony, *Career Women of America, 1776-1840;* Marshall Jones Co., 1950.

Doggett, Laurence L., *History of the Y.M.C.A. in North America;* Association Press, 1951.

Douglass, H. Paul, *Church Unity Movements in the United States;* Institute of Social and Religious Research, 1934.

Drummond, Andrew Landale, *The Story of American Protestantism;* Beacon Press, 1950.

Ferguson, Charles W., *A Little Democracy Is a Dangerous Thing;* Association Press, 1948.

Fry, C. Luther, *The U.S. Looks at Its Churches;* Institute of Social and Religious Research, 1934.

Garrison, Winfred Ernest, *Religion Follows the Frontier;* Harper, 1931.

Graham, Billy, *Revival in Our Time;* Van Kampen Press, 1950.

Hall, Thomas Cuming, *The Religious Background of American Culture;* Little, Brown, 1930.

Hanzsche, Wm. Thomson, *The Presbyterians. The Story of a Staunch and Sturdy People;* Westminster Press, 1934.

Hay, Clyde Lemont, *The Blind Spot in American Public Education;* Macmillan, 1950.

Hough, Lynn Harold, *The Dignity of Man;* Abingdon-Cokesbury, 1950.

Jenney, Ray Freeman, *I Am a Protestant;* Bobbs-Merrill, 1951.

Johnson, Alvin W., Frank H. Yost, *Separation of Church and State in the United States;* Univ. of Minnesota Press, 1948.

Johnson, Raymond B., *What Is Happening In Religious Education;* Beacon Press, 1948.

Latourette, Kenneth Scott, *A History of the Expansion of Christianity,* 7 vols.; Harper, 1937-1945.

Latourette, Kenneth Scott, *Missions and the American Mind;* Foundation Press, 1949.

Lindquist, G. E. E., *The Red Man in the United States;* George H. Doran Co., 1923.

Lotz, Philip Henry, *Orientation in Religious Education;* Abingdon-Cokesbury Press, 1950.

Luccock, Halford E., *Christian Faith and Economic Change;* Abingdon Press, 1936.

Luccock, Halford E., Paul Hutchinson, *The Story of Methodism;* Methodist Book Concern, 1926.

McNeill, John T., *Christian Hope for World Society;* Willett, Clark, 1937.

Mathews, Basil, *Forward Through the Ages;* Friendship Press, 1951.

May, Henry F., *Protestant Churches and Industrial America;* Harper, 1949.

Mead, Frank S., *The March of Eleven Men;* Grosset & Dunlap, 1931.

Mead, Frank S., *See These Banners Go;* Bobbs-Merrill, 1934.

Moore, John F., *Will America Become Catholic?;* Harper, 1931.

Morrison, Charles Clayton, *Can Protestantism Win America?;* Harper, 1948.

Moss, Leslie B., *Adventures in Missionary Co-operation;* Foreign Missions Conference of North America, 1930.

Mott, John R., *Five Decades and a Forward View;* Harper, 1939.

Munro, Harry C., *Be Glad You're a Protestant!;* Bethany Press, 1948.

Murdock, Kenneth B., *Literature & Theology in Colonial New England;* Harvard University Press, 1949.

Nichols, James Hastings, *Primer for Protestants;* Association Press, 1947.

Nichols, James Hastings, *Democracy and the Churches;* Westminster, 1951.

Niebuhr, H. Richard, *The Kingdom of God in America;* Willett, Clark, 1937.

Parker, Everett C., Eleanor Inman and Ross Snyder, *Religious Radio;* Harper, 1948.

Pauch, Wilhelm, *The Heritage of the Reformation;* Beacon Press, 1950.

Peattie, Donald Culross, *American Heartwood;* Houghton Mifflin, 1949.

Perry, Ralph Barton, *Puritanism and Democracy;* Vanguard Press, 1944.

Poling, Daniel A., *A Preacher Looks At War;* Macmillan, 1939.

Stifler, Francis Carr, *Every Man's Book;* Harper, 1941.

Stokes, Anson Phelps, *Church and State in the United States,* 3 vols.; Harper, 1950.

Sweet, William Warren, *The American Churches;* Abingdon-Cokesbury, 1948.

Sweet, William Warren, *The Story of Religions in America;* Harper, 1930.

Taft, Charles P., *Why I Am for the Church;* Farrar, Straus, 1947.

Thomas, Elbert D., *This Nation Under God;* Harper, 1950.

Van Dusen, Henry P., *World Christianity: Yesterday, Today and Tomorrow;* Abingdon-Cokesbury, 1942.

Wallace, Paul A., *The Muhlenbergs of Pennsylvania;* University of Pennsylvania Press, 1950.

Washington, Booker T., *The Story of the Negro,* 2 vols.; Doubleday, Page, 1909.

Weigle, Luther A., *American Idealism;* Yale University Press, 1928.

Worrell, Edward K., *Restoring God to Education;* Van Kampen Press, 1950.

Yearbook of American Churches; edited by Geo. F. Ketcham for Federal Council of Churches, 1949.